GRETA GARBO

GRETA GARBO

A Pyramid Illustrated History of the Movies

by
RICHARD CORLISS

General Editor: **TED SENNETT**

PUBLICATIONS
NEW YORK

GRETA GARBO

A Pyramid Illustrated History of the Movies

First edition published July, 1974

ISBN 0-515-03480-0

Library of Congress Catalog Card Number: 74-1567

Printed in the United States of America

Pyramid Books are published by Pyramid Communications, Inc. Its trademarks, consisting of the word "Pyramid" and the portrayal of a pyramid, are registered in the United States Patent Office.

Pyramid Communications, Inc., 919 Third Avenue, New York, N.Y. 10022

graphic design by anthony basile

TO *MY OWN MYSTERIOUS* LADY
who taught me all I know . . .

ACKNOWLEDGMENTS

For extraordinary generosity in facilitating my viewing of many MGM Garbo films: Doug Lemza. For the rewards of friendship and scholarship: Charles Silver, Stephen Harvey, Molly Haskell, Elliott Sirkin, Ray Durgnat, William Yushak, and Andrew Sarris. For the marvelous stills: Jerry Vermilye. For other reasons: my wife Mary, whom I met six years ago at a Garbo retrospective.

CONTENTS

This is a book about the art of an actress and the craft of her films. To say this is to speak heresy—for isn't film the art of the director, and aren't performers merely so many caged lions and chorus girls? At the highest and most personal level of the medium, perhaps. But movies are acted as well as directed. The actor may be speaking the writer's dialogue, may be coached in each gesture, may be photographed with Rembrandt's eye. We may sense the fluttering hands of a dozen cosmeticians just off-screen, and know that a canny editor has orchestrated it all into a small opus of rhythm and light. It's true: others create the illusion. But the reality—sometimes naked, sometimes sublime—is that of the actor.

A second heresy: movie acting is the only acting that can be talked about critically. The great performers of previous centuries might as well be figures from a folk tale, for we have no evidence on which to base a discussion of their art—the art, as Edwin Booth defined it, of "a sculptor who carves in snow." A similar problem exists for actors on the modern stage. Theater is, after all, a kind of group hallucination, and theater criticism a journalist's report of a seance. Since the production inevitably ends, there is only memory to rely on. And what could be more fickle than the memory of a theatrical illusion?

THE ART: THE ACTOR AS CREATOR

The least we can say about screen acting is that, forced by the properties of the medium, it dares to be seen and judged by posterity. We can talk precisely about Mary Pickford's work, and not about Sarah Bernhardt's, because Bernhardt is a myth and Pickford a fact. The twenty-first-century moviegoer won't have to read books like this to discover how Hollywood stars looked and talked, and acted. In a feat of true movie magic, he will simply open a tin coffin, and the dead will awaken—all talking, all singing, all dancing. Whether he finds the spectacle absurd or superb, he will be able to decide, for himself and his age, how good our movies really were.

It's hard to guess what our buff of the future will think of movies, "the director's art." But it's possible that he will realize that acting is also an art. The Cagney walk may again be as famous as the Lubitsch touch. Retrospectives of Katharine Hepburn movies will function as raw material for dissertations on a talent greater even than Cukor's. And perhaps actor criticism—without suppressing the fan's instinct that keeps luring us back to the

movies—will become something more than star-gazing. We dream about stars; we should think about them too. And no Hollywood performer offers more challenging food for thought than the actress the Europeans call "La Divina"—Garbo.

Other books have traced every known fact of Greta Garbo's biography, from her birth in Stockholm in poverty on September 18, 1905 through her discovery by director Mauritz Stiller and her appearance in his film, *The Saga of Gosta Berling* (1924), to her arrival and immediate triumph in Hollywood—and on to the mysterious life she has led since retiring in 1941. But this book is about Garbo's life on the screen. It's a study of her beauty and talent as it shone through her twenty-five extant feature films. To the degree that the millimeter naunces of great screen acting can be calibrated, this book will attempt to do so—to provide a biography of the Garbo legend from the best evidence we have: her films.

When we think of Hollywood movies in their Golden Age, what do we remember and love? Not the tasteful adaptations of masterworks from other media, but the crazy originals: the contemporary melodramas and musicals and screwball comedies. We prefer the gangster movies and yellow-journalism exposés to the stately costume pictures and leftist morality plays which the studios were forever patting themselves on the back for producing. That's why most people today, looking back at the three major studios of the thirties and forties, respond to the mile-a-minute syncopation of Warner Bros. and the elegant foxtrot of Paramount, and start to yawn when the Metro metronome ticks in their memories.

Sitting through a typical batch of MGM movies produced under the aegis of Irving Thalberg is like being locked up in one of the porcelain rooms of the Victoria and Albert Museum. The artifacts are refined but the atmosphere is stifling. There were hidden pockets of refreshing raunchiness in the Thalberg three-piece suit—the Jean Harlow movies, for example—but, for the most part, its *Reader's Digest* attitude toward High Art makes today's filmgoer grateful for the philistine vulgarity of the other studios. After an evening of MGM product, you want to go to a roller derby.

THE INDUSTRY: MR. THALBERG AND MR. HAYS

When MGM took over stars from another studio, the irresistible impulse would be to sanitize and domesticate them. Just compare the funny-spunky Jeanette MacDonald of *Love Me Tonight* (Paramount) with the sickly-sweet MacDonald of *Rose Marie* (MGM), or the anarchic Marx Brothers of *Duck Soup* (Paramount) with the cuddly Marxes of *At the Circus* (MGM). Garbo, who was wooed from UFA, the great German film factory of the twenties, seemed to resent the change MGM wreaked on her—in the other direction. "I am not vamp," she is reported to have said in 1928. "In Germany, I play sweet, innocent girls . . . . Never am I wicked type. Here they say yes, I am. I do not like."

In the three decades between Bram Stoker's novel and Bela Lugosi's incarnation of the demon, the male vampire was shortened to the female vamp. Theodosia Goodman changed her name to Theda Bara, and developed the movies' first negative image of the D.W. Griffith virgin princess. Whether or not the sudden popularity of the vamp spoke to the subterranean paranoia of America's

PETER THE TRAMP (1923). Garbo's first feature film, made in Sweden

native-born poor at a peak moment of Central European immigration, the fact remains that the most successful vamps of the twenties were exotic foreigners. Garbo was cast in this mold. And in *The Temptress* (1926), reverberations of Stoker's vampirism were audible in a toast "to the temptress, who asks for nothing—but takes everything a man can give—and more."

There were other strong social currents for the young actress to swim against. In movies of the twenties, no less than today, homoerotic friendship (emphasis on friend) was often more highly prized than heterosexual love (emphasis on sex). Of course, Hollywood was only underlining a traditional American trait. The greatest and most indigenous American authors of the nineteenth century—Melville, Twain, Cooper—wrote of men who lived without women. Our contribution to world literature was the Western. We were a country of pioneers, and our heroes were soldiers and trailblazers.

Women were not allowed in this locker-room pantheon. They found themselves simplified into two extreme stereotypes: the schoolmarm and the whore. Garbo was no schoolmarm—she possessed an electrifying presence that could lend substance to roles created out of cardboard and convention. Her characters did some unbelievable things, but we always believed *her*. She was intelligent and beautiful; whatever she did, she must have had a reason.

MGM had cast Garbo to type—and "type" was something approaching a religion with Thalberg. As her type was the flaunter of conventions, her doom was assured in Reel One. Pascal said it first, but if there had been room on the MGM scroll, Thalberg would have inscribed it there: "It is superstitious to put one's faith in conventions, but it is arrogant to be unwilling to submit to them." Maybe that's why a mediocre Paramount comedy is easier to take today than a mediocre Metro costumer: MGM took the conventions seriously, and Paramount didn't. Those conventions are dated today. The films that respected them are dated too.

The studio seemed to favor novelists like Hermann Sudermann and Vicente Blasco-Ibáñez. Both writers enjoyed stoking the passions of their characters (and their readers), and then throwing a bucket of natural or divine retribution on the sinners. The water was not holy but cold, and it was used not to absolve but to punish. You can see why the studios—and their censorship czar, Will Hays—would go for this formula. It titillated moviegoers to fever pitch, and then sanctimoniously crossed its legs. The Hays Code's motto might have been

THE TEMPTRESS
(1926). With Antonio Moreno

LOVE (1927). A scene from the abandoned version, with Ricardo Cortez and Lionel Barrymore

Rasputin's: sin so ye may repent. And there was a second premise: the more attractively ye sin, the more spectacularly ye must repent.

Garbo, whose talent for conveying and arousing passion verged on the hypnotic, was thus forced to endure some pretty heavy climactic suffering. The finales of her early films are a catalogue of Draconian vengefulness: she goes mad, drowns in a frozen pond, throws herself under the wheels of an onrushing train (in the original final print of *Love*), and drives smack into a tree. It's true that death was speedily followed by resurrection—in her next film. But only, like the phoenix, to live again in order to die again.

Throughout her career, Garbo struggled against all of these conventions, which seem to have been designed for the sole purpose of providing Hollywood movies with dramatic tension. Because Garbo was so often a great actress, and because she so rarely worked with great directors, these conventions are especially unworthy as antagonizing forces. Garbo was a true goddess, if ever the cinema had one. She deserved to be struck down, not by some fustian social custom, but by the gods, by a fate that was inevitable rather than just predictable.

Perhaps Garbo was her own, and only, ideal antagonist, and the great Garbo role would have traced a descent into madness. Three of the screen's forceful personalities were given this chance—Anna Magnani in *The Miracle*, Vivien Leigh in *A Streetcar Named Desire*, and Katharine Hepburn in *Long Day's Journey into Night*—and responded to the challenge with three supreme performances. But except for the end of *The Temptress* (made when Garbo was nineteen), and a single episode in *A Woman of Affairs* (made when she was twenty-two), Garbo was never given a "mad scene" worthy of the name.

That she made, so early in her career, so much of these meager opportunities, suggests what she might have done with a decent mad role ten years later, in the fullness of her beauty and art. Robert Taylor has said of Garbo that "she thought with her eyes"—and one can easily imagine her mind's light going out behind those eyes, can see the beauty of her intelligence drop like a shrug from her face, can hear the deadened voice say, in Eugene O'Neill's most magical cadences: "I fell in love / with James Tyrone / and was so happy / for a time."

Instead, Garbo fell in love with Count Vronsky and Lieutenant Rosanoff and Baron von Geigern and Captain Karl von Rhaden and even Napoleon. She suffered and died and was redeemed—sometimes all in the same movie. And, much of the time, she gives the impression of a Paderewski doing finger exercises, a Pavlova walking through her roles. She "walked" divinely—but we are saddened to know that she rarely danced. Not that Garbo herself was to blame: most of her scripts were typed with one finger, and in one key. And the subjects Thalberg chose for her often acted as a ball and chain around our ballerina's feet.

Garbo was a valuable property at MGM. Even after *Queen Christina* (1933), when her mass popularity began to wane, her films continued to gross well in Europe. And the prestige she wore like royal robes was a palpable, if not bankable, asset for the studio. Thalberg obviously respected her, and must have thought he was serving his star nobly by using the works of O'Neill, Tolstoy, Maugham, Pirandello, Dumas, and the like. Unfortunately, Thalberg's attempts to legitimatize movies by applying a varnish of classical literature gave many of her films the comfortable but musty smell of Victorian stuffed furniture.

Thalberg's prize entries in the Respectability Sweepstakes were Garbo and Norma Shearer. If Shearer was in fact Thalberg's wife, Garbo was in effect his European mistress. The two stars shared the studio's tonier projects: both essayed O'Neill and Adela Rogers St.

RETA GARBO

At movie premiere with Norma Shearer, Irving Thalberg, and John Gilbert

John; Garbo played Napoleon's mistress one year, Shearer played Marie Antoinette the next. There is even some evidence that the studio originally signed Garbo as Shearer's continental alter ego: the earliest MGM publicity dubbed her "the Norma Shearer of Sweden."

It seemed that, for Thalberg, the greatest thing he could do for his star actresses was to turn them into Ladies. With Shearer it couldn't have mattered much: she might have been a great lady, but she was never a really good actress. But Garbo, because she had much more to give, had much more to lose by being placed in one epic of antique nobility after another. It's not that Garbo needed roles of majestic tragedy—she certainly got enough of those!—but she showed, in films as slight as *The Mysterious Lady* (1928) and as substantial as *Ninotchka* (1939), that she could have fun without sacrificing the sense of fated seriousness that made her roles, and sometimes even her films, something special.

But before we decide to deface Thalberg's grave (or picket the movie version of *The Last Tycoon*), we should admit that Garbo *needed* MGM. It offered a motherly bosom for this least secure of superstars. And though, early in her career, Garbo held out for seven months until her projects were upgraded from Sudermann to Tolstoy, she seems to have found her later pablum congenial enough not to make a fuss over. She even vetoed a David O. Selznick proposal to do the hit play *Dark Victory* with a screenplay by Philip Barry. This meaty, contemporary role might have helped her in 1935; instead she insisted on remaking *Anna Karenina*. The decision hurt Garbo, but not Bette Davis, who scored a triumph in the role at Warners in 1939.

The result of all these forces —Thalberg's protectiveness, the public's image of a star, her own complacency—was that Garbo made fewer good films than any major performer, and almost no films (*Ninotchka* being the probable exception) that would have been good without her. But if her movies are not art, they are Garbo. And if you look closely, you can trace the creation of a beautiful young woman from a chubby Swedish starlet, and the flowering of a great actress in the Culver City hothouse.

It's been said that her movies were "Garbo vehicles," but the reverse is true: it was Garbo who carried her films. She was a Rolls-Royce with a second-class cargo (her scripts) and no driver (director). If, as is generally thought today, film is the art of the director, then Garbo's films were not art. More often, they were the art of the art director: glossy bits of frou-frou, assembly-line entertainments that lacked even the naive energy of a Warners musical or a Universal horror show.

Molly Haskell has written that Garbo was able "to survive . . . good and bad directors and bad and awful leading men." Survive, perhaps; thrive, perhaps not. Garbo's tragedy was that her closest professional relationship was not with a great director, or even a sympathetic writer, but with cameraman William Daniels, who photographed all her Hollywood films except *The Temptress* (1926), *The Single Standard* (1929), *Conquest* (1937), and *Two-Faced Woman* (1941). She also relied heavily on Cedric Gibbons, the MGM art director, and Gilbert Adrian, who designed her costumes. It's as if she was more concerned with her image than with her films' impact.

Garbo ran through the MGM stable of directors, most of whom were talented hacks. In 1933 Dwight Macdonald wrote, "Garbo has only once in her Hollywood

THE OTHERS: DIRECTORS AND LEADING MEN

career had a first-rate director—Feyder, who made *The Kiss*" (1929). Marcel Carné had written of Jacques Feyder: "He dreams of bringing to the screen such-and-such a satirical farce or such-and-such a conflict between workers and management, but found it necessary always to have recourse to a romantic story." Certainly MGM would have it no other way, and *The Kiss* was just a bubble, graceful but insubstantial.

The one director who stands out in Garbo's filmography—because of quantity, not quality—was Clarence Brown, who directed seven of her films. Brown's mentor had been the innovative French-born director, Maurice Tourneur; and Tourneur's distinctive visual style, extravagant and arch, left an elegant aftertaste on Brown's palate that lasted throughout the silent period. *Flesh and the Devil* (1927) and *A Woman of Affairs* (1929), his two silent Garbo films, have a *mise-en-scène* as complex and witty as almost anything late-twenties Hollywood produced.

Brown has recalled that he "used to direct her very quietly. I never gave her a direction above a

CONQUEST (1937).
As Marie Walewska

whisper." In the sound era, and especially with Garbo, his films became as discreet as the stage directions he gave his star. By receding beneath the MGM patina of Good Taste, he surrendered the reins of visual authorship to Daniels and Gibbons. And, because he no longer imposed himself on the material, the films themselves became less imposing. The gloss was still there, but the glow was gone.

FLESH AND THE DEVIL (1927). With John Gilbert

Other directors had equally erratic track records with Garbo. George Cukor directed her greatest film, *Camille* (1937), and one of her worst, *Two-Faced Woman* (1941). Fred Niblo, who had made a mess of *The Temptress*, did a fine job with *The Mysterious Lady*. And the directors who might have helped her were kept away from her. Ernst Lubitsch had told Garbo as early as 1932 that he'd love to make a film with her; but when he was loaned to MGM in 1934, it was to make *The Merry Widow* with Jeanette MacDonald. Not until 1939, three years after Thalberg's death, could Lubitsch provide a revivifying touch of sophisticated comedy to Garbo's dour image: *Ninotchka*.

By the nature of this book, Garbo's leading men must seem like so many male concubines in her central-casting harem. By the nature of her films, they seem mostly like eunuchs—at best, prince consorts to a snow queen. It's hard to

THE TEMPTRESS (1926). As Elena

AS YOU DESIRE ME (1932). With Melvyn Douglas

say whether they, or their scripts, or their directors are to blame, but the general impression is that they are pleasant enough as dancing-school partners, but hardly the sort who could, with complete sexual authority, sweep Garbo off her feet and into their arms and out of a stuffy masked ball. They project domestic gentility, and a certain embarrassment in the presence of this fated force of nature, this Garbo. They came to her as princes and, like a beautiful, wicked fairy, she turned them into frogs.

The effect she had on them could be devastating. The pressure of her personality was often too great to be borne. They became claustrophobic, obsessed with escape. So away they ran: to Argentina, Egypt, China, Java, nameless exile —anywhere. It's as if they realized how quickly their characters and selves were fading in the audience's eyes, how much their identity was being reduced to the "Garbo leading man"—and so decided they'd be missed more in their absence than if they just hung around, appendages to a lady star's mystique.

If Garbo's silent-screen co-stars come closer to holding their own, it's because the early Garbo was passionate—she had to play those perfervid love scenes with *somebody*. But as her career developed, and the shadow of her myth lengthened, she discarded the physical for the metaphysical. Many of her greatest love scenes were played with herself, or with

THE SINGLE STANDARD (1929). With Nils Asther

A WOMAN OF AFFAIRS (1929). With John Gilbert

props: the flowers in *A Woman of Affairs*, the furniture in *Queen Christina*, a handsome but wooden Robert Taylor at the end of *Camille*. She was in need less of leading men than of altar boys. So the actors were neutered before they ever walked on the set.

There were exceptions, of course. Melvyn Douglas, demolished in *As You Desire Me* (1932), recovered seven years later and, in *Ninotchka*, kept his equilibrium by not taking Garbo too seriously. John Barrymore, in *Grand Hotel* (1932), and Charles Boyer, in *Conquest* (1937), come close to outshining Garbo, though she recovers in the middle of *Grand Hotel* and takes Boyer down with her in *Conquest*, sunk by the script. Conrad Nagel seems to enjoy himself in *The Mysterious Lady;* George Brent brought respect but not awe to his role in *The Painted Veil* (1934); Nils Asther's sensual masculinity made him an attractive lover in *The Single Standard;* and Clark Gable wasn't cowed by *Susan Lenox: Her Fall and Rise* (1931).

But the great exception was John Gilbert, her co-star in *Flesh and the Devil*, *Love* (1927), *A Woman of Affairs*, and *Queen Christina*. When we think of Gilbert today, we tend to remember only his dazzling smile and his tenor voice—which audiences of the time laughed at because it didn't match his baritone good looks, and which doomed his career in the sound era. But Gilbert was more than white teeth and a white voice. He was a great star *and* a fine actor; his performance in the 1926 *La Bohème*, with its dizzying emotional arpeggios, stands as a pinnacle of silent screen acting.

If Garbo was unattainably mythic—a flat-chested fertility goddess susceptible only to our adoration—then Gilbert was the boy next door as seen through the dreamy soft focus of puppy love, or mother love, or hero worship. He was the best that America could think of the boys it had raised: dashing, kind, faithful, and incurably romantic. It was inevitable that this star of the Roaring Twenties would fall madly in love with a Swedish siren, and just as inevitable that, when the country awoke to a decade-long hangover called the Depression, Garbo and America would reject him along with yesterday's worn-out dreams.

THE FACE: GARBO'S SILENT FILMS

If the cinema of Hollywood's Golden Age was America's communal dream, then to watch old films on television is to review, under a movieola microscope, the clumsy passions and crazy fears of ourselves, our parents, and our movie-mad nation. And to see, for example, Henry Fonda in *The Grapes of Wrath* interrupted by a commercial of Henry Fonda selling GAF film, is to imagine the Orson Welles of today playing the old Charles Foster Kane—and the Welles of some future day being filmed as he mutters, for the last time, "Rosebud." The movie vault is an archive of icons, a time machine which, simply by reminding us how beautiful and young our surrogate dreamers were, can't help but evoke darker dreams of our own: images of aging, and shadowy premonitions of death.

It's odd to watch an actress, in random television showings of her films, ricochet backward and forward in time like some fourth-dimension handball. But for the historian with a streak of ghoulish curiosity, it helps fix the various stages in her career. There's a period, just at the portals of middle age, when an actress is still insisting on playing young women—Ingrid Bergman in *Under Capricorn* is a good example. The mask of youth is clearly cracking, and it's not a pleasant spectacle to watch unless we realize that in her subsequent films with Roberto Rossellini, Bergman's child-mask fell off and revealed the lovely, knowing face of her maturity. Today, age and the elements have burnished her face, like an ancient outdoor sculpture, and created another mask: strong, smiling, and serene.

Garbo made her last film when she was thirty-five and still a matchless beauty in the twilight of her young womanhood. But great changes had taken place since she was first recorded on film. In a 1921 "commercial" for a Stockholm department store, we see a plump, giddy girl modeling three dresses; in a promotional film made the following year for a line of bakery products, this same undistinguished girl gorges on a cream puff, and then greedily grabs some cookies. A photograph taken the same year shows the girl with her sister Alma, who closely resembles the Garbo of *Flesh and the Devil.* It's not until Mauritz Stiller and the Irving Thalberg body shop took this chunky girl in hand that the mist of corpulence clears—and out walks Garbo.

Several years pass. Teeth are capped, eyebrows plucked, hair re-

styled. And suddenly, around the time of *The Mysterious Lady*, we come face to face with the breathtakingly beautiful Garbo whose youthful splendor will endure for the rest of her career. This is the Garbo we shall stare at, stupefied and adoring; the divine pinup every fan will hang on the fourth wall of his sentimental soul; the woman who will stoke nitrate fires that haven't yet gone out. When, in *The Mysterious Lady*, a Russian officer proposes a toast to "Tania the Beautiful," today's audience ecstatically seconds the toast—and drinks a champagne, vintage 1928, that is both perfectly aged and impossibly new.

THE SAGA OF GOSTA BERLING (1924)

LARS HANSON: *Where are you going, Countess?*

GARBO: *I was looking at the fire.*

As a grandiose distillation of the first Golden Age of Swedish film, *The Saga of Gosta Berling* might be worth an entire chapter in a history of the silent cinema—if only it could be seen in its entirety. Mauritz Stiller, famed for his intense melodramas and subtly wicked comedies, took a Selma Lagerlöf novel and threw images from it onto his celluloid canvas with the force and color of a Jackson Pollock. But more than an hour of the original four is missing from the most complete extant print, and the version circulated in the United States is a mere 105 minutes.

So we must content ourselves with the briefest appraisal of the film, and concentrate on the bud we know will flower into Greta Garbo. Gosta Berling is a rather average young man who is too much the lecher to be a good priest, and too much the priest to be a good lecher. After passing through poverty and disgrace as a pensioner in the mansion of a Swedish nobleman, he ends up (at least in the American version) betrothed to a young Italian countess. The original film must have been a rousing popular entertainment, with its orgies, "screen scenes," renunciations, mother's and daughter's curses fulfilled, and a girl who literally dies of heartbreak. No wonder Hollywood wanted Stiller!

The actors with the two shortest names in the cast went to Hollywood too. As Gosta, Lars Hanson has the adolescent impetuosity of the young Douglas Fairbanks, Jr. and the Don Juan fatalism of the Swedish actor Jarl Kulle. Hanson also has a searing stare that could burn through celluloid. In *Gosta Berling* it was the stare of a defrocked minister asserting his spiritual superiority over the gentry who ignored or feared him, but MGM would put that gaze to work

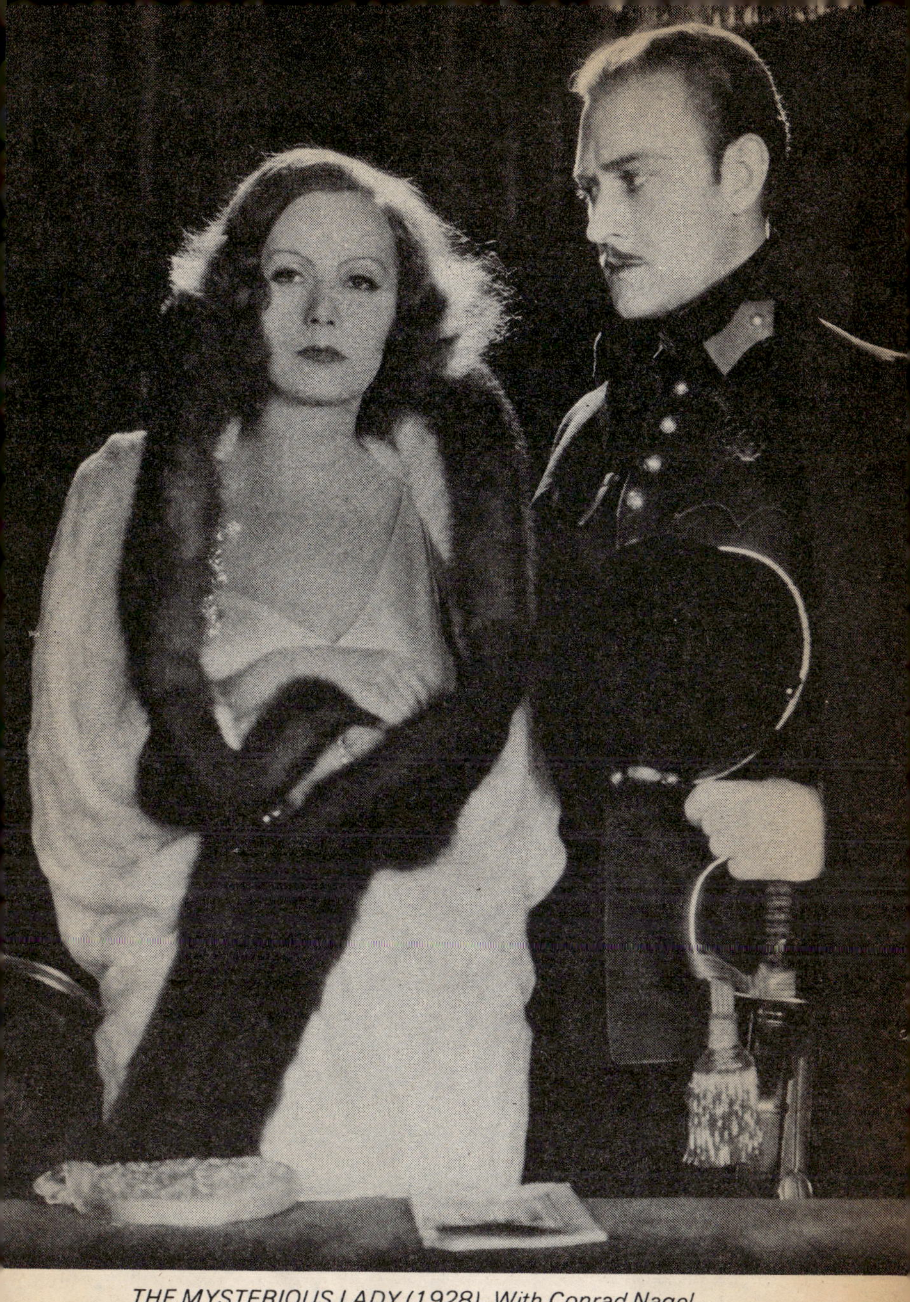

THE MYSTERIOUS LADY (1928). With Conrad Nagel

on the likes of Lillian Gish, Marceline Day, and (in *Flesh and the Devil* and *The Divine Woman)* a divine devil named Garbo.

Stiller had given Greta Gustafsson her new name, but not yet a new personality—or looks. He had made her lose twenty pounds for the role, but she is still perhaps twenty pounds heavier than she will be by the time of *The Torrent*. If, because of her Latin surname and Italian role, we should think of a Fellini actress she resembles, it is not the gaunt and galvanizing Anouk Aimée but rather the plump, hoydenish Sandra Milo. Stiller tried to help her, having her talk in profile with her head raised to conceal that extra chin. Unfortunately, nothing can conceal her flabby arms.

But if Stiller failed as a dietician,

THE SAGA OF GOSTA BERLING (1924). As the Countess

he shone as a prophet. What he obviously saw in Garbo were those eyes—impressive enough when she was young and heavy. Later they dominated her face; even here they take your breath away. Perhaps he also spotted, with a starmaker's X-ray eyes, the perfect bone structure beneath that chubby face. He might have seen it—we do today—in the brilliant night sequence when Gosta abducts her for a sleigh ride across a frozen lake.

This is star quality we are discussing, of course, not the art of acting. To hold, say, Bette Davis and Humphrey Bogart responsible for their performances in *Bad Sister* (1931) would be unfair: their talent was undefined, their command of the medium slight, their control over scenarios nonexistent. Garbo

THE SAGA OF GOSTA BERLING (1924). With Lars Hanson

JOYLESS STREET (1925). With Jaro Furth

was only seventeen when she made *Gosta Berling*, so it's best to look at her not as a critic with scalpel in hand, but as an old family friend flipping the pages of a baby book, looking at pictures of an ungainly child who turned into one of the most beautiful women in the world.

There *is* a great actress in the film: Gerda Lundeqvist-Dahlström, as the lady of the manor who is disowned by her mother and her husband, and who gives sage counsel to both Hanson and Garbo. When Garbo drops desolate at her knee, Lundeqvist-Dahlström consoles the nervous neophyte—as a character and an actress—the way Garbo would later help Elizabeth Young in *Queen Christina.*

And when Lundeqvist-Dahlström tells us, "I was once called the beautiful Margaret Celsing; I loved and was loved in return," she seems magically beautiful for a moment, and then ravaged again—an act of sorcery Garbo will perform at the end of *Anna*

Karenina. Finally the lovely old woman's face falls into a repose that is both slack and resolute, as she says, "And I go on living." Here, at least, Garbo was different: ever the romantic pessimist, she is all too willing to die from love, or remorse, or a divinity's exhaustion from living in an alien world.

JOYLESS STREET (1925)

HE: *I'm madly in love with you. How can I convince you?*

SHE: *Get rich.*

In the Marxist monster movies of postwar Germany *(Caligari, Mabuse, The Golem)*, money buys you sex, and sex buys you money. *Joyless Street* plays some intriguing variations on the theme that obsessed Weimar filmmakers, and it wears its charnel elegance jauntily. But if G.W. Pabst's villains are comically complex—running through all the colors of a Stygian rainbow—his heroines must make do with paper thin souls and lace valentine hearts. And Garbo is one of the heroines.

She comes off as a Gish maiden without the angelic hysteria, and without the universe of crazy idealism that Griffith spun protectively around his star. Seeing Garbo as a one-dimensional saint is almost enough to make us look forward to her MGM roles as a two-dimensional vamp. Saintliness, however perverse, is rarely as interesting dramatically as sinfulness, since the only thing that can happen to it is defilement under the horny hands of an equally horny villain. In Hollywood, at least, Garbo was allowed to play the extraordinary woman fighting to fit into—or escape from—the straitjacket of common morality.

So we look at *Joyless Street* not for what it offers, but for what it promises. A decade after it appeared, the English critic James Agate saw the young Garbo's "face which, lacking the putty-like, dimpled prettiness of your normal film star, resembled a portrait roughly limned with only the eyes finished. . . . In *Joyless Street* Garbo is all that a film star in the making should be . . . to the critical eye the hardly begun symphony of Garbo's acting is worth more while than any other scene complete to its last double bar."*

Halfway through the film, this rough portrait catches its own eye in the first of Garbo's many confrontations with a mirror. For the older Garbo, the mirror was an emblem of analysis rather than narcissism. Molly Haskell has called the actress "her own sexual opposite"; the mirror is both lover and parent, critic and confessor. In *Joyless Street* she looks lovingly into a full-length mir-

*James Agate, *Around Cinemas*, London, Horne and Val Thal, 1946, p. 150

THE TORRENT (1926). With Arthur Edmund Carewe

ror as she models the kind of fur coat she will wear as comfortably as a negligee in her Hollywood films.

Fifteen years later, we can find her, as Ninotchka, sitting before another mirror and staring at herself bemusedly in Bolshevik gray and a "ridiculous" Parisian hat. And we know that, in a few seconds, she will ask her suave lover if "I don't look too foolish?"—and underline that plea with all the insecurity of a poor girl from Stockholm who discovered herself playing queens and courtesans in the movies.

THE TORRENT (1926)

"If you love me not,
Then I'll love you.
If I love you–
Then beware."

—sung by Garbo

The scene is the Madonna's shrine behind the Moreno home in Valencia. And the kneeling acolyte—who prays "that the voice which God had given her might bring wealth and ease to her parents"—bears a striking resemblance to the young Vivien Leigh, elf-maiden of Tara. It is, in fact, Greta Garbo in her first scene in a Hollywood movie. *The Torrent* is remembered, if at all, simply as Garbo's first film at MGM, but it deserves better than that. Not only does it prefigure many of the morals and motifs of her later pictures, but it avoids many of those films' pirouettes into the ludicrous. All things considered (the times, the material, the studio), *The Torrent* is a surprisingly adult piece of work.

If the Nobel Prize for Literature

were selected by heavy-breathing housewives, Vicente Blasco-Ibáñez would surely have won it during his reign in the twenties. Certainly MGM would have been happy to nominate him. *The Four Horsemen of the Apocalypse*, *Blood and Sand*, and *Mare Nostrum* had been among the studio's greatest successes; and now Garbo, their latest discovery, was being granted the honor of starring in Ibáñez adaptations as her first two projects. *The Temptress*, the second of the two, typed her as The Vamp You'd Love to Date—a characterization that stuck to her, like no-smear lipstick, throughout her early eminence. In *The Torrent*, though, her Leonora is believably two-dimensional: round and flat at the same time.

The clichés are all here, clipped to our heroine's bosom as securely as the spray of orange blossoms that symbolizes her love for Don Rafael Brull (Ricardo Cortez). *The Torrent*'s triangle is rich boy, poor girl, meddling mother; vows are sworn on rosary beads, love letters are full of pleas and renunciations; and the textual subtitles are a bit fulsome: "Then a torrent—as furious and relentless as the passion that surged in the hearts of the lovers." But you'll find these in most films of the period, including works by Griffith, Chaplin, and Murnau. Monta Bell, director of *The Torrent*, wasn't quite in this class, and neither is the film. It is, however, much more than a program feature, and Garbo's performance is more than a creditable debut.

When the film begins, Cortez is a pillar of the lower aristocracy, and Garbo a flower of the lower class. At first, her status is too meager for Cortez to consider marrying her; later, when she has gone to Paris and become "La Brunna," an opera star with her own recording company and a score of fawning swains, the caste roles are reversed. Cortez had rejected the music of Garbo's spheres for bureaucratic respectability, the siren song of the bourgeoisie. At first, the new star sees her only love as a figure of fun, preening about his election as town deputy before a woman who is now the queen of Upper Bohemia. But soon her remembered romance fans into a passion that will keep flaring up for the rest of their lives.

Though out of her element and separated from Mauritz Stiller, Garbo gives a fine performance, full of feeling and technical precocity. Her first Hollywood kiss is one to remember. As she listens to Cortez's love murmurs, her face falls into a modified swoon: mouth half-open, eyes half-closed. Cortez kisses her—and her expression doesn't change in the slightest. To the dreamer, a "dream come true" may also be a dream; if she moves a muscle, she may find herself embracing the air. Later, she is more aggressive, and we find the lovers in the oddly contorted position that will become traditional in Garbo movies: she above, he below; his head in her lap, her head on his chest.

There are, to be sure, moments early in the film when Garbo works too hard with her eyes: overstating emotions instead of expressing them, dropping nuances like anvils, registering filial devotion or kewpie-doll concupiscence in broad, tremulous strokes. But she grows in the role, as if this Swedish peasant girl was more comfortable playing a character that looked forward to the legend she would become, rather than one that reflected the milieu she had escaped. By the final scenes, when she faces the stooped and graying Cortez—a Dorian Gray inspecting her own picture—she is utterly convincing as an actress and a star. And the film is wise enough to leave her, uncertain, in solitary splendor. The celluloid mirror for once is a crystal ball.

As her character's star rises, and her costumes grow more opulent and more outrageous, Garbo seems to age with each scene into later incarnations of herself. After her first success, she is adorned in tiger fur and a butch haircut—and her face (if not her coiffure) looks

THE TORRENT (1926). With Ricardo Cortez

THE TORRENT (1926). With Ricardo Cortez

wrenched from the frames of *Love*, made two years later. When she returns home as a star, she is for the first time completely beautiful, almost as she will be in *The Mysterious Lady.* Later still, she's cool, beautiful, and alone, with a headdress (made of what appear to be strips of aluminum foil) and a demeanor suggestive of *Mata Hari*.

The effect is amazing: it's like seeing a retrospective of her development as a film beauty before it actually happened. By the end of *The Torrent* her face seems more severely contoured, her eyes more glacially clear, her head tilted upward by the chinstrap of spiritual pride. The phenomenon is that of a star creating her own myth within the time-space of a single film. But *The Temptress* will set her back on square one.

THE TEMPTRESS (1926)

GARBO: *May God forgive you—for all you have done for me.*

However myopic Thalberg may have been, he wasn't blind to press clippings and box-office statements. So in her second American film, Greta Garbo's name came above the title—and ahead of Antonio Moreno's. More important to Garbo was the director assigned to *The Temptress:* Mauritz Stiller. But, though Stiller's influence on his star never wavered until his death in 1928 (and perhaps not even then), their mutual romance with the studio ended abruptly. Ten days after shooting began, Stiller was fired.

It's tempting to imagine Stiller in Moreno's role, smothering Garbo with open-mouthed closeups, creating a soft-focus effect with some rapturous heavy breathing on the camera lens; and to think of Thalberg as the pimping husband who barges in on their lovemaking and throws Our Hero out. But maybe it's not as simple as that; *nothing's* as simple as the plot of a Garbo film. There are stories of Stiller shouting "Stop!" when he wanted his cameraman to start shooting, and "Go!" when he wanted them to stop. Whatever the reasons, Thalberg eventually said "Stop," and Stiller was gone, to be replaced by Fred Niblo, who had saved *Ben Hur* the year before, and who now "saved" Garbo from her mentor, confessor, and creator.

In a 1926 letter to some Swedish friends about the film, Garbo says that she wants to "apologize to everyone for it. Terrible, the story, Garbo, everything is so rotten. It is no exaggeration—I was below criticism." Not quite. To say that Garbo is the best thing in the movie is to damn with faint praise, but there are moments—sculpted, one would like to think, by Stiller—when her radiance can be seen behind the obscuring curtains of

THE TEMPTRESS (1926). A scene from the abandoned Mauritz Stiller version

plot, supporting actors, and moral conventions.

There are other moments when it seems she's trying to get through those curtains by chewing them in the worst ham-actor tradition. Her ecstasy—as opposed to her passion—is still a set of rigid mannerisms, and not yet the expression of an incandescent soul. You can almost hear the director's instructions in words of one syllable, and you can see Garbo reacting with gestures that are painted on, like Pinocchio's smile. The lips part slowly, in a cartoon of lust; a thousand Lilliputian stagehands raise those asbestos eyelids (and take their time about it); the eyes roll mechanically back and forth, evoking the spirit of Betty Boop. This is the vamp as camp. It's what people who don't like silent movies remember of them: unfelt intensity, glamour without craft.

And yet—when discussing even the worst Garbo films, there is always an "and yet"—it is still easy to see why she became a star in so short a time, and with such flimsy filmic support, and why, when the subtitle proclaimed, "You are beautiful!" a million lip-readers nodded in agreement. For the film's first sequence, Stiller has got her up in her *Gosta Berling* costume, and it doesn't flatter her: too much white on white. But, at age twenty, she remarkably projects a sense of exhaustion—until Moreno plucks her from a maelstrom of masquerading revelers. Her white eye-mask hides nothing (the one beneath it is more impenetrable); and once she removes it, she seems to have shrugged off the last vestige of her evening gown, the last shred of an inhibition.

She surveys Moreno's face with her hands—as if she had never before experienced hunger, and now realizes she's been hungry all her life—and kisses him full on the mouth. It's hard to convey the effect of this kiss, except to say that it's not a Hollywood euphemism for passionate lovemaking, but rather the love act itself. Linda Lovelace has only got the words down; Garbo knows—has composed—the music. We sometimes forget that before Garbo became the Divine Masochist, whiplashed by fate, she had been a certified Sex Goddess. After seeing Reel One of *The Temptress*, we are unlikely to forget it again.

Even with all that heavy breathing it's hard to understand exactly why Garbo's Elena is thought to be so evil. As a satanic pestilence, she's rather passive, usually standing around looking gorgeous while infatuated men toss their hearts at her feet like quoits. Is she to blame for her beauty, or their foolishness? As well blame a magnet for attracting arrant filings! Garbo's real problem is that she lives by a moral standard held too high for men to reach—so they grab what they can touch: her body. When told that she has ruined the lives of half a dozen men who would do anything for her, she replies bitterly: "Not for me, but for my body. Not for my happiness, but theirs."

Garbo wanders through most of

THE TEMPTRESS (1926). With Antonio Moreno

THE TEMPTRESS (1926). With Antonio Moreno

her early films like a world traveler without a passport, renting her body out to many men but pledging her love to only one. To her, sex is a pleasant time-killer, marriage is a nonbinding contract, but love is a sacred vow. "I told you I loved you," she says to Moreno. "I have never said that to any other man." But Moreno can't accept the idea of a madonna who's not also a virgin; he wants retroactive rights to her body as well as universal rights to her soul.

To diagram the plot of *The Temptress*, you wouldn't draw an eternal triangle, but rather a straight line (Garbo at one end, her doom at the other) with several irrelevant tangents. There's Marc MacDermott as her husband, who farms her out to a randy banker for some spare change; Lionel Barrymore as a worker driven to jealous murder by the very sight of Elena; and, most ludicrous and enjoyable of all, Roy D'Arcy, with his John Gilbert smile gone berserk, as the mad Argentine gypsy who loses a sadistic bola fight to Moreno.

By the end of the film, Garbo has reached the end of her line. We find her, crazed and diseased, sitting in a Paris cafe, at last pursuing the trade men have been teaching her for so many years. Like Tennessee Williams' Blanche DuBois, she had gotten on the wrong streetcar: not ecstasy but desire. And, like Blanche, she has a devastating curtain line. When Moreno tries to remind her of their great love (which was really only hers), she replies, vaguely, "I meet so many men"—and wanders away, down another street. Perhaps, if we give *The Temptress* more than it is due, we will remind ourselves of the film's opening quote (from Tagore), and wonder how close this melodrama could have come toward a genuinely tragic irony: "Oh, Woman! Thou are not alone the Creation of God—but of men!"

FLESH AND THE DEVIL (1927)

JOHN GILBERT: *Who . . . are . . . you?*

GARBO: *What does it matter?*

GILBERT: *You are . . . very beautiful.*

GARBO: *You are . . . very young.*

Garbo had turned twenty-one during the making of *Flesh and the Devil;* Gilbert was thirty-one. But it's Gilbert whose spirit leaps like an intoxicated song-and-dance man, and Garbo who seems to paraphrase Portia and say, "My great heart is aweary of this little world." As so often, we find her at one of those functions—here it's a military ball—which the aristocracy uses to ritualize its boredom. If Love is for Garbo the first and only commandment, Tedium is the first deadly sin.

Of course she is married, of

FLESH AND THE DEVIL (1927). With Marcelle Corday

course to a no-count count, and of course it will end in a duel. But the night and Gilbert are young; and Garbo, at this "larval" stage in her development as a love object, is just beautiful enough to kiss if not to possess, to hold if not to have. Their first love scene—with Gilbert as Adam and Garbo as the most delectable fruit in a garden of heavenly delights—gives off the sparks of two novas colliding head-on, high in the night sky, celestial and spectacular. Their last love scene, six years later in *Queen Christina,* will be of a quieter, more melancholy combustion: a shooting star and a falling star grazing each other on the way to their separate eternities.

Everybody writes this way about Garbo and Gilbert. Read Clarence Brown on the subject: "I am working with raw material. They are in that blissful state of love that is so like a rosy cloud that they imagine themselves hidden behind it, as well as lost in it." In *Flesh and the Devil* Brown adeptly juggled three dramatic tones—comic, platonic, and passionate—not only juggled them, but bounced one off the other. Throughout the first part of the film, Brown's injections of earthy humor keep the swollen carcass of plot alive, or at least lifelike. And, as the "serious" sections continue their descent into the Valley of Hokum, the comic touches become defter and more illuminating—as when we are told who the winner was in a duel between Garbo's husband and Gilbert: by the slight smile on her face as she tries on a chic mourning hat.

Brown's sophisticated comic touches needed no explanations, but the morality behind Hermann Sudermann's story-line needed something—perhaps an apology. Sudermann was a German novelist whose works described the struggle between Good (yay!) and Evil (boo!) in terms that Savonarola would have found simple-minded. But Hollywood loved him: he was the Teutonic Blasco-Ibáñez. In 1927 it made two films from Sudermann stories: *Flesh and the Devil* and *Sunrise.*

The commercial cinema is notorious for turning great novels into Classic comic books on celluloid. But more than once it has alchemized dross like Sudermann's into highly polished silver *(Flesh and the Devil)* or pure spun gold *(Sunrise).* Both films set up a pair of good people threatened by an evil interloper. In *Sunrise,* The Man and His Wife struggle against the wiles of The Woman from The City. But in *Flesh and the Devil,* Garbo herself is The Woman from The City, and the virtuous couple is played by John Gilbert and Lars Hanson!

In a marathon of indecisiveness,

FLESH AND THE DEVIL (1927). With John Gilbert

Garbo falls in love with Gilbert; then, when Gilbert leaves the country after his duel, she marries Hanson ("he was so kind"); then, when Gilbert returns, she has an affair with him and begs him to flee with her; then, when Gilbert agrees, she says they should stay and continue their tryst clandestinely; then, when Hanson discovers them at play, she lets her new husband and her lover fight a duel (again!); then she changes her mind and tries to stop it, and dies on the way.

It is no small achievement to lend coherence to a character whose life-plan changes at least once a reel, but for the most part Garbo manages it, because her desperate love for Gilbert informs every caprice. And if we call Gilbert the most inspired of her leading men from this period, it is be-

FLESH AND THE DEVIL (1927). With John Gilbert and Marc MacDermott

cause he alone convinces us that he deserves that love. More miraculously, he convinces us of the rightness of his comradely love for Lars Hanson. As the similarity of this triangle to the one in *Sunrise* makes clear, Gilbert is simultaneously carrying on two different love affairs—and two *kinds* of love affairs—and it takes most of the film before he realizes that the two cannot coexist peacefully.

During the argument that leads to their duel, the two men meet, at opposite ends of the film frame. Gilbert's face is suddenly quite lined; Hanson's is serene in the purity of his anger. Gilbert's hand rests on his friend's shoulder, as if to say, "Please, let's talk, before you throw away two lifetimes of friendship"; when Hanson's eyes suggest no possibility of compromise, Gilbert's hand discreetly falls away.

If the title and moral of this film are to be believed, Gilbert is cursed by weakness of the flesh, and Garbo by the power of the devil. As a meddlesome minister intones to Gilbert, "When the devil cannot reach us through the spirit, he creates a woman beautiful enough to reach us through the flesh." If to be sensual is to be satanic, then Garbo was certainly a demon. During the sermon at a church service, she applies her lipstick; later she drinks from the Eucharistic cup voluptuously, even as she makes love religiously. In one love scene with Gilbert, she grips his legs fiercely; in another, she lays her left forearm naturally but provocatively over her right breast.

Gilbert finally surrenders, not so much passive as transfixed, and we too are literally charmed as we watch Garbo (in Parker Tyler's words) "slither over her men like a starved python." It is a case of the snake entrancing the snake charmer, and it will happen many more times in her silent films until, around the time of *Anna Christie*, Garbo sheds her snakeskin for a more suitable garment—a shroud of mystery. In her later films, every word and gesture will suggest that love affairs are only a way of marking time before the crucial assignation: not with the Devil, but with Death.

LOVE (1927

It is over now. I am quite alone.

The story was "Anna Karenina."

LOVE (1927). With John Gilbert

But after the stars of *Flesh and the Devil* had ignited box-office returns and gossip columns with their lovemaking on- and off-screen, MGM couldn't resist heralding "John Gilbert and Greta Garbo in *Love.*" (A year later, they would resist keeping the title of John Colton's original story, which would have resulted in the billing: "Greta Garbo in *Heat*"—and settled for the safer *Wild Orchids.)* Critics would say it was just as well: *Love* bore little relation to "Anna Karenina." But novels and movies are two different forms, and it's just as well that the twain rarely meet.

Tolstoy, Sudermann, or Ibáñez, the conflict was the same—adultery, the bourgeois tragedy—and so, almost, were the scenarios. Again, as in *The Temptress* and *Flesh and the Devil*, the hero meets and falls in love with Garbo without realizing that she is married. Here they meet, in a reprise of the most memorable scene in *Gosta Berling*, on a snow-covered plain, and ride over the ice to a convenient inn. Inside, the ice turns to fire: in the lovers' den there are two hearths, two candelabra, and, as Gilbert gets his first good look at Garbo, he burns his fingers on a match. But for the first time, the Garbo of *Love* rejects her hero's advances—for a moment, which for Gilbert is a lifetime of frustrated anticipation.

To Garbo's lovers, she is an obsession; to her husbands, she is only an ornament. And as soon as we see a Garbo husband, we know whether the film considers it right or wrong that she should leave him for someone else, and tragic or triumphant that she return. The answer is in the actor's face: it tells us whether he's good (sexless but sympathetic) or bad (sexless and cruel). Art historians would call this "iconography"; we'll call it typecasting. Because Marc MacDermott (her husband in *The Temptress* and *Flesh and the Devil)* and Brandon Hurst *(Love)* have deadened eyes and sewn-on scowls, we know they are bad. Because Lewis Stone has a Mount Rushmore profile, and crinkles instead of wrinkles, we know he's good. Exchange Stone for Hurst, and *Wild Orchids* would become a tragedy, while *Love* would offer Garbo a fascinating dilemma.

As it is, Hurst as Karenin seems initially the only sensible husband Garbo has had so far. Of course, their sex life is a distant memory, if not a downright delusion—we feel that their son must have been born through divine intervention—but, to his credit, Karenin doesn't object when his wife falls in love with Count Vronsky. "I may find it more convenient not to know," he tells her. "I shall do nothing sensational [until] you have . . . made public

LOVE (1927). With Philippe De Lacy

LOVE (1927). As Anna

your guilt." Soon enough, the affair goes public, and the pair of lovers heads for foreign parts—where a child resembling the true love of Anna's life, her son Sergei, propels her back home, out of Vronsky's arms.

Tolstoy had written in his novel that "All happy marriages are more or less dissimilar; all unhappy marriages are more or less alike." As the Anna-Vronsky family liaison begins its interminable bickering, it comes more and more to resemble the marriage she had deserted. Anna had been able to live (before Vronsky) without a real husband, but she cannot exist now without her son. And in dramatizing this problem, *Love* suggests overtones Tolstoy may not have dreamed of. For Gilbert, however cuddly and cherubic, can never be a son to Garbo; but Philippe De Lacy, as Sergei, is almost treated as a lover.

This may sound like acute critical fantasy, but anyone who has seen the film will have noticed the strange erotic tension between Garbo and De Lacy. Garbo was, after all, only twenty-two when she played this mother of a ten-year-old boy. And De Lacy, who had already appeared in more films than Garbo, knew how to project a pre-Raphaelite sensuality that made him the perfect love object for a repressed and doting mother. This attraction may have been written between the frames, but if it escaped contemporary audiences, it is plain enough to modern ones.

When Anna and Sergei meet after a long separation, he takes her head in his hands—and kisses it from above, in patented Garbo style. She offers many loving pats on all four cheeks. Before and beyond Gilbert, De Lacy provides Garbo with a safe sexual outlet —safe because sanctified by marriage! Though the difference between *Love* and the 1935 *Anna Karenina* may be said to be the difference between Gilbert's boyish energy and Fredric March's sullen righteousness, it could also be expressed as the difference between Freddie Bartholomew in the remake and Philippe De Lacy here: between an asexual fawn and an androgynous satyr, between Peter Pan and pagan Pan.

To discuss this subplot at all is perhaps to underline the understated. Certainly Gilbert is no "cover" lover—he's sexy enough in his own right, and his love scenes with Garbo are just as adroit, if not so steamy, as those in *Flesh and the Devil*. He radiates the supreme, and earned, assurance of a great star in love with his leading lady. One wishes that—as with Stiller at the moment of his sailing for America with Garbo in his luggage—the reader could pause with Gilbert and help him savor his glory without realizing that everything would soon be extinguished: his stardom, his co-star, and, last of all, his smile.

Garbo herself does a disappearing act following *Love*. Through an accident of film history, her next film, a fictionalized life of Sarah Bernhardt directed by Victor Seastrom, and called *The Divine Woman*, no longer exists. So we shall never know exactly how divine Garbo was in the story of an actress whose lover (Lars Hanson) goes to jail for her sake. It is a secret she shared only with the audiences of her own time.

THE MYSTERIOUS LADY (1928)

I came here your lover. I leave —your enemy!

The Mysterious Lady is vintage nonsense, and most welcome. It offers us our first real opportunity simply to gaze at Garbo without having to avert our gaze from the suffocating seriousness pecking at her from both sides of the frame. It's the most enjoyable of her silent films, a lighthearted barnstormer of a show. It even parodies (in a dialogue between two soldiers) the opening plot movement of several Garbo films: ". . . and just as we were about to kiss, her husband

THE DIVINE WOMAN (1928). With Lars Hanson in scene from lost film

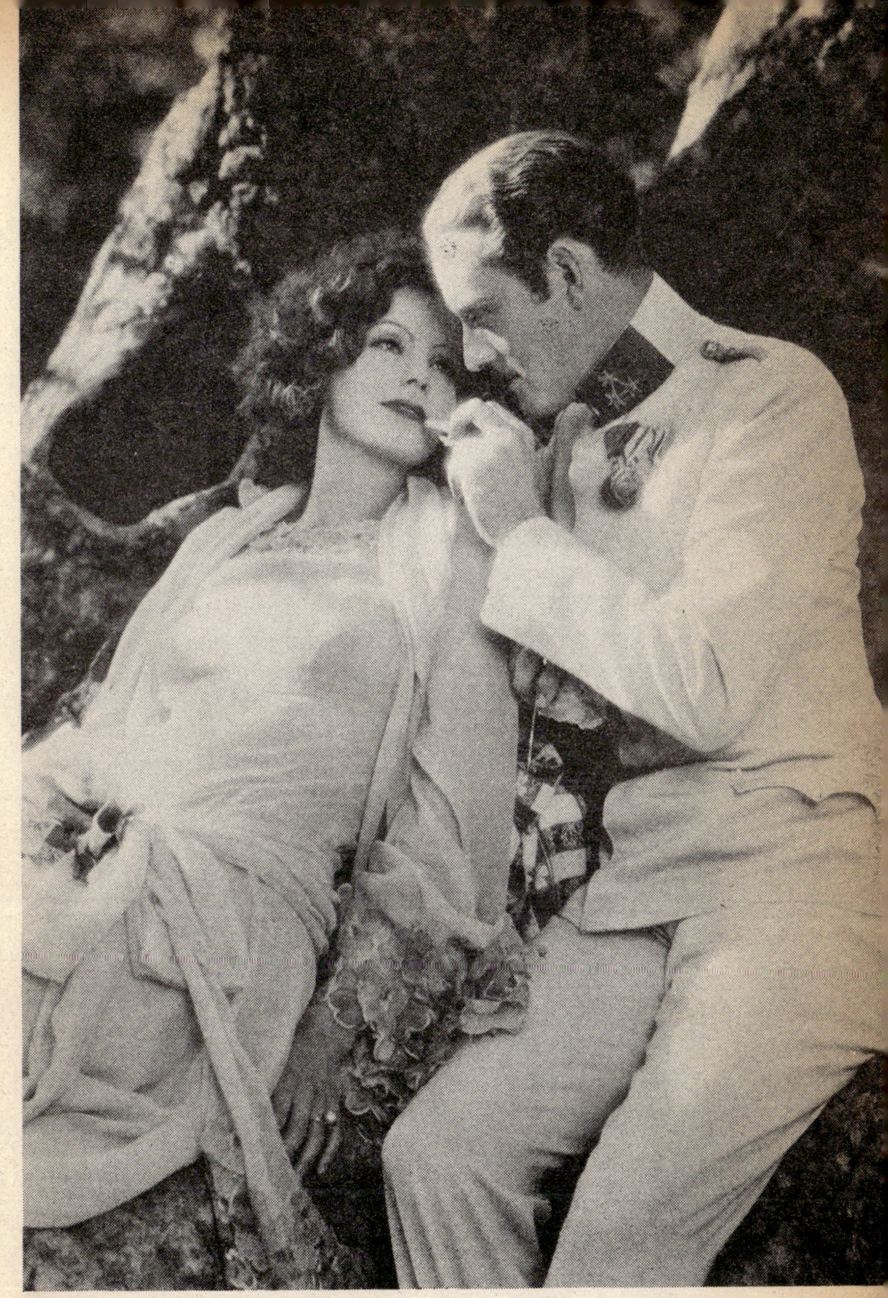

THE MYSTERIOUS LADY (1928). With Conrad Nagel

burst in—and pulled down the shades!" Garbo herself has a good time here, relaxing between appointments with Hays-ordered doom. And, in this slight film, we can see intimations of the kind of sophisticated comic actress she might have become if MGM hadn't set her adrift in a score of motheaten melodramas.

Her first scene is a little joke on herself. We find her (as often) at the opera, and (as always) tired, her head resting languidly on her arm. When brave and true Austrian officer Conrad Nagel steps into her box, she pretends it's a mistake, but her gestures tell us otherwise. They are more open than usual, maybe even reckless: she brazenly drapes her arms on the chairs behind her as she speaks to Nagel, exaggerating the arc of her breasts, and we realize that this Garbo is not tired but tiger-tense in anticipation of her noble, vulnerable prey.

Already she is playing our expectations of her character against themselves—one of the nicest nuances an actor-star can create. Later on, after we learn that Garbo-Tania is a Russian spy (a playful prototype of her Mata Hari), her gestures sustain the halo of mystery around our lady; if not downright Delphic, these gestures are at least ambivalent. When she stares Nagel down with a half-condescending, half-encouraging smile, we wonder what she is telegraphing to him: "Come hither" or "Go yon"? It's the message of a first-class spy, for it won't be decoded until several reels later—when she falls in love with him.

In other respects, Garbo makes a terrible secret agent. Her boss (Gustav von Seyffertitz), who plays the traditional role of "the husband" in earlier Garbo films, is a master spy insanely (and understandably) possessive of his mistress-spy. But when Garbo falls for Nagel, and determines to spirit him and herself out of Russia, she plies her trade with all the aplomb of television's inept secret agent Maxwell Smart, with long-winded notes smuggled to her lover, and guilty looks at her suspicious boss. And when von Seyffertitz discovers her double-cross, he mouths one of the drollest of silent-screen subtitles: "I taught you all you know, Tania, but I didn't teach you all *I* know!"

But Tania Hari has an ace up the sleeve of her Adrian gown: she shoots von Seyffertitz, who falls dead into an old-fashioned easy chair whose high back faces the outside door; one of the junior spies knocks on that door and asks what to do with the captured Nagel; when he opens the door, he sees Garbo sitting on her boss-lover's leg, and one well-tailored von Seyffertitz

THE MYSTERIOUS LADY (1928). With Gustav von Seyffertitz

sleeve resting familiarly in her lap; Garbo says something to the unseen face, seems to listen to a response, then tells the adjutant, "The general says, 'Send him in, alone.' " The ruse works—and provides an audaciously entertaining commentary on the vocation of espionage: to kill a lover, to romance a corpse.

Fred Niblo, the time-and-motion specialist who had directed the less interesting two-thirds of *The Temptress*, presides over *The Mysterious Lady* with busy but easy authority. And the film is filled with the sort of felicitous touches one almost took for granted at the end of the silent era—when, just as it had perfectly learned the vocabulary of a complex sign-language, it was declared inoperative. To dwell on our star's later career is to be even more grateful to *The Mysterious Lady*. For once, we didn't have to genuflect in front of the Garbo grotto, or curse the infidels who consigned our smiling goddess to the marketplace of bourgeois tragedies.

A WOMAN OF AFFAIRS (1929)

HOBART BOSWORTH: *You are young, Diana. You will fall in love again.*

GARBO: *How little you know of love—my kind of love.*

The opening subtitle calls *A Woman of Affairs* "the story of a gallant lady—a lady who was perhaps foolish and reckless beyond need—but withal a very gallant lady." Ninety minutes later, we find ourselves wishing that Garbo had been a little less gallant, John Gilbert a good deal less reckless, and the film a lot less foolish. Adapted and sanitized from Michael Arlen's "scandalous" book, *The Green Hat,* this movie version blurred the novel's focal point

A WOMAN OF AFFAIRS (1929). With Lewis Stone

by changing a major character's venereal disease into kleptomania, and the "purity" he had supposedly died for into "decency."

Even the names of the characters were changed; the Hays Office must have thought that the very sight of "Iris March" or "Dr. Conrad Masters" on the screen would have lured millions of impressionable moviegoers toward the heartbreak of syphilis. The dialogue was similarly starched and laundered: Douglas Fairbanks Jr., who plays most of the movie in a glazed, disheveled twilight state halfway between Jekyll and Hyde, looks madly into Garbo's eyes, and shouts (in a subtitle), "You—!"; and Garbo turns to her onlookers and asks numbly, "Did you hear what he called me?" It was perhaps at this moment that Garbo's employers realized it was time to put their star into talking pictures.

Garbo was a genuine box-office phenomenon by now, and the studio responded to this fact by finding more sympathetic parts for her. But in *A Woman of Affairs,* instead of placing Garbo and her lover against the world (as in *Love*), they made her the only important sympathetic character. Her husband is an all-American (or all-English) phony with a hidden talent for embezzling. Her brother is a neurotic idealist who turns against her, like a vindictive Bambi, when she pretends to the world that her husband died "for decency." And her own true love (Gilbert) walks out on her—or passively lets her walk out on him—five times during the movie!

The film begins nicely, with the two stars for once radiating a domestic lovelight: the natural affection of longtime, loving friends instead of the passion of star-crossed lovers. In the early scenes, Gilbert easily and artfully conceals his own memory of a burnt-out affair with Garbo as well as his knowledge of what doom the script has in store for him. And Garbo makes something natural and savory out of the bourgeois pleasures of falling and being in love.

This mood can't last. Hollywood saw quiet love scenes like these simply as interludes between a mad clinch and an angry crunch. Conflicts were the stuff of the cinema, to be resolved with the most tattered formulae of nineteenth-century melodrama. So, for a start, Gilbert's father (Hobart Bosworth) lectures him on the honor of his poor-but-respectable ancestors. In Old Hollywood, family honor was taken just seriously enough to function as an effective plot device. Here it drives Gilbert out of Garbo's arms and off to Egypt to make his fortune.

Gilbert suffers terribly from this plot ploy. After the opening scenes, he has little to do but look self-righteous and stand around flexing his jaw muscle like some unemployed moral gymnast. With his patented ebullience held in check, he's muzzled; with the cowardly turns his character must take, he's reduced to playing a human hair shirt for Garbo's sanctified masochism. Of all the Garbo men's "renunciation scenes," Gilbert's in the *Woman of Affairs* hospital scene is the prissiest and least justified. To leave Garbo in any event is to forfeit the chance to live fully, or to die exquisitely. To push her away with noodle-limp arms, when she asks only to be held close, makes Gilbert's character not only vapid but stupid.

Idiocies proliferate. Garbo and Gilbert refuse to say "I love you" to anyone else, but marry others anyway. Garbo's unloved husband throws himself out of the marital bed and a convenient window because the police have discovered his crime—and then the police tell no one about it. Garbo accepts a

A WOMAN OF AFFAIRS (1929). With John Gilbert

seven-year plague of abuse simply to keep a secret that would bother no one except her brother. The lad falls into a fatal dissipation, and dies at the *exact moment* Garbo and Gilbert consummate an adulterous affair. Finally, when her name has been cleared, she picks up an ace of spades and, suddenly superstitious, decides to kill herself by driving into the tree she and Gilbert had sworn their love under.

Faced with a plot as convoluted and predestined as a Chinese ballet, what can Clarence Brown do but direct actors like traffic? He simply discards the flamboyant eroticism of *Flesh and the Devil* and concentrates as much as possible on elaborately paired shots, some of them half a film apart, which subtly reinforce, or undercut, the story's plodding ironies. A character looks out a window, or shakes hands in a gentleman's pact; lovers kiss; a ring falls off the heroine's hand—and we feel, through Brown's *mise-en-scène*, the reverberations of a Hollywood-drawn fate.

A WOMAN OF AFFAIRS (1929). With Douglas Fairbanks, Jr.

As this lace curtain of doom draws more closely around her, and her sphere of movement becomes more confined, Garbo resolutely takes over. Liberating her character from its entrapping scenario by a combined effort of beauty, talent and will, she performs genuine movie magic. Of Garbo's death in *Camille*, Cecelia Ager had said, "You can sense the precise moment when her lovely spirit leaves her fascinating clay." Here, when Garbo learns of Fairbanks's death, you can feel the air chill around her, and see her life-spirit escape, like condensed breath, from her depleted body as it sinks to the floor.

A reel or so later, Garbo is lying unconscious in a French hospital after suffering a nervous collapse. The flowers Gilbert has sent her have been removed from her room. As Gilbert paces nervously in the hospital corridor, with his loving but unloved wife in tow, Garbo suddenly appears. She sleepwalks down the corridor and, in a single swooping gesture that is one of the great moments of silent passion, removes the flowers from their vase and clutches them to her breast. "I woke up—and you weren't there," she murmurs to her love surrogates. "I don't want much—only you."

Here we can see one of the most majestic transformations in the cinema: from acting to being, from pulp to poetry. Like most of the Garbo "set pieces," this aria is a solo. With only a melodramatic situation, a jug of flowers, and herself, Garbo convinces us that she is incarnating the spirit of Greek tragedy instead of Michael Arlen. It's a minute of screen acting that by itself makes *A Woman of Affairs* one of her most imposing achievements. Something beautiful has been created out of almost nothing—which is less a case of skating on thin ice than of walking on water.

WILD ORCHIDS (1929)

NILS ASTHER (to Garbo): *You are like the orchids of your country—you have the same cold enchantment. In Java the orchids grow wild—and their perfume fills the air.*

Lewis Stone might have been John Gilbert's father. The bone structure is more sepulchral, the demeanor more domestic, the smile more reassuring—but there's a strong family resemblance all the same. Put it another way: he's a Gilbert who's solid instead of sexy. So the Garbo who would be expected to love him—and resist the advances of a handsome young prince because of that love—must be a slightly different Garbo. In many another scenario, the situa-

WILD ORCHIDS (1929).
As Lili Sterling

WILD ORCHIDS (1929). With Nils Asther

tion would be reversed; for in *Wild Orchids*, Stone's character is that of a Karenin with affection, but not warmth. When she kisses, he yawns. When she touches his arm, he crosses his legs. And his final clinch of reconciliation is not a lover's burning kiss but a tepid avuncular hug.

Stone's rival (rather as fire is a rival to earth) is Nils Asther, crown prince of Java. To turn the Danish actor into an eager emir, MGM gave him slanty eyes and a Hattie McDaniel bandana for local color. But today's audience may find his soft features, apple cheeks, and cupid's-bow mouth more reminiscent of Paul McCartney—a sort of Javanese Beatle. While Stone stands about petrified, offering his wife only the quickest and most chaste of goodnight kisses, and expressing shock at the thought that he might have to sleep with her in a double bed, Asther is forever astrut, looking puckish as he strokes imaginary chin whiskers that will never grow. A sapless old man and a randy adolescent: this is the

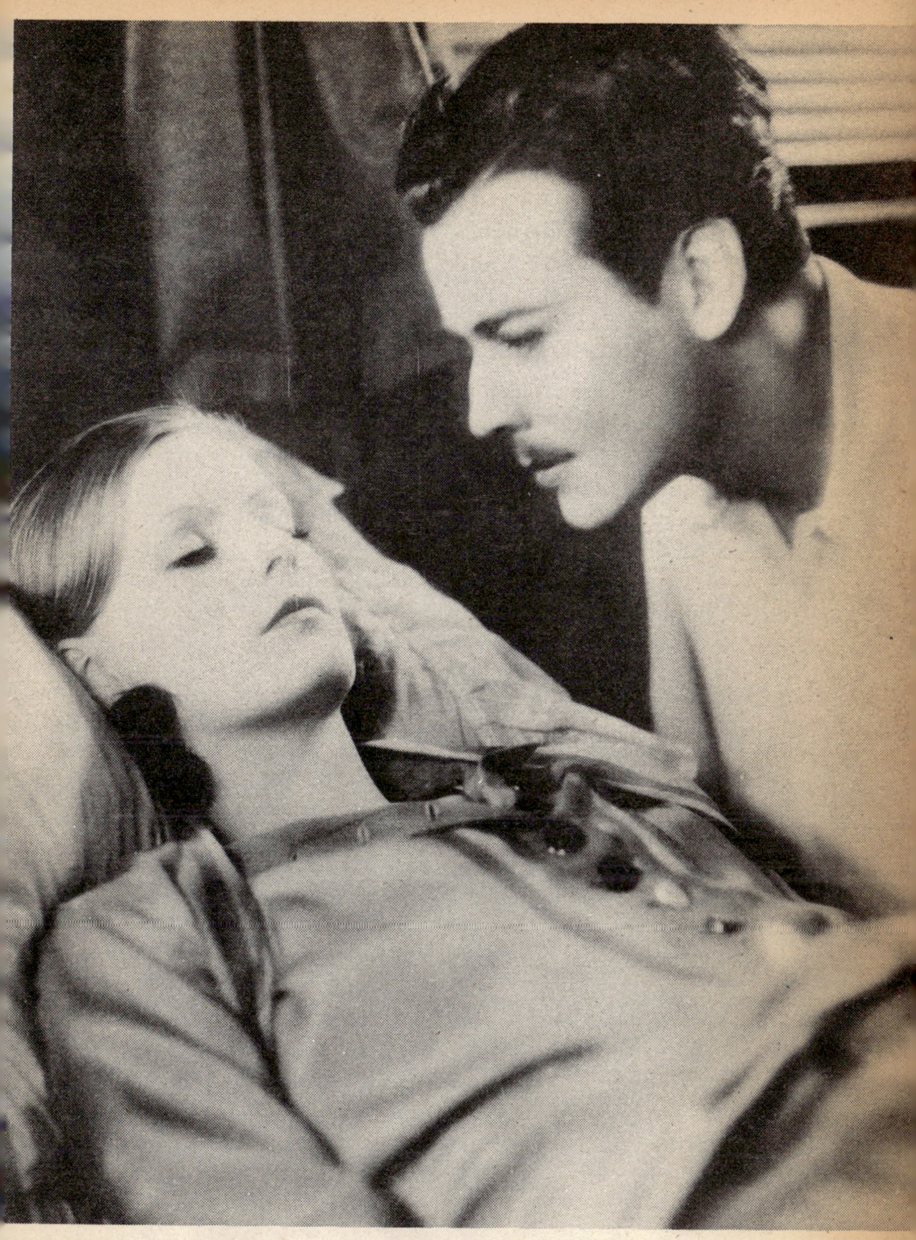

WILD ORCHIDS (1929). With Nils Asther

choice Garbo must make in *Wild Orchids*.

For the first time in her career, Garbo was working from an original film idea. But John Colton, the scenarist, had co-authored the stage version of Somerset Maugham's "Sadie Thompson" story. And Maugham had covered the same geographical and psychological area—the tropical East, humid and tumid with the spasmodic passions of repressed Occidentals—many times before. Maugham and Colton seemed to believe that temperature affects temperament; that, as Asther says here, "the heat, the everlasting heat strips everyone of all pretense." But in *Wild Orchids*, the emotions remain pent up. Garbo stays sexually faithful to a man with whom she has rarely, if ever, had sex. She ends up honoring a convention that, in her other films, she ignores or transcends: the claim of a marriage contract.

Knowing what we do of Garbo's personality, as it grows and is modified throughout her work, we must take this decision as a defeat. And Garbo gives evidence in her performance that she agrees with us. Her two most theatrical and least forgivable gestures—the nervous biting of her lower lip, and her hand running tensely through her hair—flourish recklessly here as never before. It's also in this film that we find, for the first time, her eerie ability to project spiritual

THE SINGLE STANDARD (1929). With Nils Asther

pain as a palpable ache. Her soul, hiding behind the weariness in her eyes, radiates the smoldering amber glow of a fallen angel trapped within the earthly perimeters of a bourgeois triangle.

By 1929, voice lessons and portable sound equipment were helping emancipate the talking picture from the static sibilance of only a few months before. But technical and artistic muscles were still being flexed, often tentatively, and the stray silent film was showing up its child master by going out in style. *Wild Orchids* is a gorgeous exercise, with soft-focus sunstars glistening off the actors' silhouettes, and countless tracking shots that give the impression of being an elegant if impotent nose-thumb in the face of the more earthbound talkies.

Silent films were often referred to as "shadow plays," and *Wild Orchids* is full of the frolicsome play of shadows. As Garbo stands indecisively outside Asther's bedroom door, light suddenly spills over her as the door is opened and his shadow crawls up her body; when he reaches her—and reaches *for* her, the shadow of his cupped hand falling over her breast—she retreats. Later, Garbo walks portentously toward her blind husband, and this time it's her shadow that smothers him with intimations of sexual love.

In the sound era, Sidney Franklin would become a reliable MGM house director—more house than director—and it's possible that the visual sheen of *Wild Orchids* should be credited to Daniels, Gibbons, and Adrian. If so, we can thank the studio for dressing up the production in cinematic finery, even as we blame it for having settled for the meatless bones of Colton's story: a middle-class *No Exit* where Hell is not "other people" but rather a false choice between the Devil and a deep ennui.

THE SINGLE STANDARD (1929)

NILS ASTHER (to Garbo): *I roamed through China looking for art—and found only the memory of you.*

Yet another of MGM's moral tales, *The Single Standard* puts Garbo's fidelity to the marriage bond to an even sterner test than that provided by *Wild Orchids*. Her lover is a Renaissance Man of the Jazz Age: once a prizefighter, now a famous painter. Their love is strong and true, and their only quarrels would seem to be over who is the more gaudily noble of the two. When they decide on the obligatory separation, it's because of his concern for her reputation. And then—for a reason known only to Adela Rogers St. John, the author, and Will Hays, the censor—Garbo gets married and has a child. When her lover returns, she opts for duty over desire, and he sails away forever: a male Queen Christina, with impotent chagrin as his only companion.

The linchpin for this queer reversal is the baby. The Hays Code commandment on adultery went like this: if you have a bad husband, you can leave him; if he gave you a child, you have to stay—because it means you've had sex with him (so you're not pure for your lover), and because the child must have a mother. Complicating matters in *The Single Standard* is Garbo's callow husband, John Mack Brown, who had committed suicide (for decency) in *A Woman of Affairs* and threatens it again here. To save one life and nurture another—or to live with her love—this is the choice she must make. Or, rather, which Hays made for her.

So all that's left to savor is the sexual sparks set off between Garbo and Nils Asther, the pomaded Punjab of *Wild Orchids*. Their affair takes place on Asther's yacht, ominously named the *All Alone;* and when Garbo leans back into his lap, and Asther holds on to her naked arms as if they were oars, he is both caring and commanding. You want to sign him to a lifetime contract, just to keep him around for moments when Garbo's other lovers turn righteous or spineless. And you can understand why Garbo seems so at ease here, in her first "100-percent-American role." *The Single Standard* is a small film, and toward the end it turns small-minded; but when the two lovers are together on the high seas, you can see in Nils Asther that rare star whose romantic light is as bright as Garbo's.

THE KISS (1929)

Half us women would shoot our husbands—if only we had the nerve.

In its majestic twilight, the silent cinema was generating the most luscious of tonal subtleties, often in spite of its directors. Jacques Feyder's *The Kiss*, MGM's last silent film, uses its panchromatic stock to convey a wide range of gray pastels, and his camera moves with the speed and grace of a champion figure-skater. But so did *Wild Orchids*, and Sidney Franklin's directorial personality was fugitive, if not nonexistent. The only discernible difference between the two was that, for Franklin, style was an attitude; for Feyder, it was an instinct.

Like *The Mysterious Lady, The Kiss* is an elegant bit of nonsense that takes nothing seriously except the medium. If it's ultimately less entertaining than that Garbo spy movie, it may be because the genre (extramarital melodrama) boasts

THE SINGLE STANDARD (1929). With John Mack Brown

conventions that may be honored or parodied, but not treated flippantly. So Feyder's direction—straight-faced but with its fingers crossed behind its back—may strike us as condescending. Why bother to honor the conventions in the scenario but not in the *mise-en-scène*? It's possible, of course, that nothing is to be taken seriously: the screenwriter was, after all, Hans Kraly, who had written more than a score of films for Ernst Lubitsch.

The romantic geometry of *The Kiss* is unusual; a triangle involving a woman and two men, neither of whom is her husband. But Garbo's situation is the same as always. As she says to a would-be lover, "I have been a good wife to a man I don't love." In all her films, Garbo *never* had a satisfactory sex life within marriage. And in *The Kiss* her eventual affairs offer her little more excitement. The one moment of erotic electricity occurs as an accident of playfulness and willful-

THE KISS (1929). With Lew Ayres

THE KISS (1929). With Conrad Nagel

ness. When Lew Ayres, as a winsome whelp in the first throes of puppy love, begs Garbo for a goodbye kiss, she replies with the reckless bravado of a Flaubertian older woman. It's a ten-second rite of initiation into the world of adults and adultery—and it serves to seal her doom.

The sequences leading up to and trailing away from this act of self-destructive passion are merely comic prologue and melodramatic epilogue to Garbo's last epiphany on the silent screen. Feyder tracks his camera past countless people, paintings, and poodles—including a droll opening shot which follows a tour guide as he races through a museum, slowing down only slightly to indicate the occasional masterpiece. He then deftly shows how to suggest a different mood with the same cinematic syntax by tracking tragically backward as Garbo runs away from her admirer and out of the museum. Without question, Feyder knew how to make a silk purse out of a sow's ear. But when the purse contains a coin as rare as that unforgettable Garbo kiss, we must wish it had had more substantial lining.

It's also true that Garbo looks beautiful but distracted. She walks through the role as if her mind were on other things: the English lessons, the impending challenge of her first talking picture. Except for "the kiss," she brings her patented intensity to only one scene: when she seems to be looking directly into the camera, at us, smiling seraphically. The camera pulls back, and we see she is really sitting before her mirror. We realize that the camera is her mirror and we are her maids, waiting on every command this sorceress of an actress may whisper in our ears. We feel manipulated, and decide that it is time for Garbo to speak.

THE VOICE: GARBO'S SOUND FILMS

Greek tragedians, masked and heavily robed, were heard but not seen. Silent-screen performers were seen but not heard. Each group of players, acting with only part of their total equipment, focused their talents like magnifying glasses to make the viewer forget what he was missing. The words and ritualized gestures of the tragic actor created a verbal *mise-en-scène*, while the silent screen actor suggested words and worlds of meaning with an angelic smile or a tramp's shrug. "In those days we had faces," Norma Desmond says in *Sunset Boulevard.* And with faces like theirs, who needed voices?

The talkie revolution changed all that. If the beautiful face didn't have a sonorous voice to match, then both could be out of work. So Ronald Colman flourished and John Gilbert perished. Moviegoers preferred the street-smart energies of Cagney and Harlow to the rural aristocracy of Barthelmess and Gish. The Great Depression and the talkie's new realism altered movies forever, from picture poems to photojournalism. And silent actors, who had functioned as visual metaphors for emotional and moral states, now could not merely "be"—they had to do, to act, to speak English instead of the dumb-show Esperanto of a dead era.

There are those who believe that the cinema was great when it spoke that unheard universal language, before sound forced the medium to babble in countless regional dialects. To Al Jolson's prophetic line, "You ain't heard nothin' yet," the purists would mournfully answer, "We ain't seen nothin' since." It's a lament for two vanished traditions: a simpler, more idealistic America, and a unique art form that borrowed many of its effects from the stage, romantic literature, and the dance, but made out of them something new and different. *The Jazz Singer* signaled the demise of a pure strain and the birth of an unpromising hybrid.

It's true that, at first, moviemakers seemed to forget that talking pictures could also be moving pictures. But gradually the cinema took its first baby steps, and learned to walk as well as speak. Actors and directors taught themselves new vocabularies, and within a few years the art was alive and well. By 1930, two of the three major holdouts, Garbo and Lon Chaney, had made impressive talkie debuts. (Only Chaplin remained, eloquent and mute.) The ad campaign for *Anna Christie*–"GARBO TALKS!"—was succinct and successful. Hers

GARBO - Metro Goldwyn-

was truly, as Norbert Lusk wrote in *Picture Play*, "the voice that shook the world!"

ANNA CHRISTIE (1930)

Men! Oh, how I hate them—every mother's son of 'em!

Fifteen years ago, when Eric Bentley suggested that Eugene O'Neill was about as good a dramatist as his father James O'Neill was an actor—"high second-rate"—the charge seemed treasonous. Now our critical priorities have changed and, despite general respect for his late works, we find Bentley's assessment generous. Mary McCarthy has said, grudgingly, that O'Neill's plays have "a fine solidity of structure," and indeed he constructed his plays like the Eiffel Tower: leading inevitably to a dramatic point, and with all the ironwork showing. He was a playwright whose plays were not written but wrought—and, at their best, wrung from his experience.

Anna Christie, though it resembles some of his successful sea plays, is not O'Neill at his best. His insight into the female spirit was often myopic, but here it's also perfunctory and redolent of cardboard. The form of the play lacks that meticulous stagecraft that we associate with O'Neill; the tragedy is all scissors and paste, with a tacked-on happy ending. It's as if O'Neill had written *Anna Christie* only so it could be made into a Hollywood movie.

But this project was chosen as Garbo's talkie debut less for its distinguished theatrical pedigree than for its mixture of tragedy and romance, and for its heroine, with her Swedish ancestry and stoic fatalism. If MGM had treated the property with less reverence, it might have been not only an appropriate scenario but a satisfying one as well. Or perhaps Garbo simply wasn't ready for this kind of challenge. Her first talking picture was only Clarence Brown's second, and throughout *Anna Christie* you can see the star and her favorite director feeling their way toward competence.

Garbo's entrance—when she slouches into the riverfront bar, falls into a chair, and says to the bartender, "Give me a whiskey, ginger ale on the side, and don't be stingy, baby"—looks right, because she obviously took great care in altering her soignée image to conform to O'Neill's washed-out prostitute. She seems to have swallowed her chin; her tongue is dry and dirty, parched with too much life; the whole cast of her face is lower-class German instead of the usual, aristocratic woman-of-the-world. Though the photographs of these first scenes suggest a beautiful actress in five-and-dime garb, in the film itself she looks downright seedy—a true act of cinematic transformation.

If you listen to the MGM record album of highlights from Garbo talkies, you can hear a rich, lugubrious tone that breathes life into O'Neill's stammering prose. But somehow, on the screen, picture and voice don't jell. It's not the occasional mispronunciations (on the order of "the yudge told me to get a yob"); it's that Garbo's acting is pitched at the wrong level. Her Anna is a travesty of despair, and the gestures of our primal ballerina are often jerkily grandiose, as if the death throes of Pavlova's dying swan had given way to rigor mortis. To appreciate Garbo in her first talking scenes, you need to close either your eyes or your ears—only then does her performance work.

Marie Dressler tries to help. Like the best character actors, Dressler not only drew attention to herself but seemed to give confidence—acting lessons by osmosis—to the younger performers who shared scenes with her. As Marthy, the wizened wharf rat, she's an Emily Post of drunken dignity, with a cartoon bulldog face that makes a perfect match for George F. Marion, who plays Anna's negligent father. In other respects, Dressler acts rings around Marion. But what can you do with a role that forces you to

ANNA CHRISTIE (1930). With Marie Dressler

ANNA CHRISTIE (1930)
As Anna

repeat the line "that old devil sea" more than a dozen times in a seventy-four-minute film?

Once *Anna Christie* escapes into the fog-shrouded sea, it becomes freer and less ponderously metaphysical, like so many of O'Neill's autobiographical characters, from the sailors in *The Long Voyage Home* to Edmund Tyrone in *Long Day's Journey into Night*. And Garbo, in a new hairdo and a simple sweater and skirt, becomes a new woman—a real woman, alive and in love with a fog that "makes me feel as if I was out of things altogether . . . as if I'd been living a long time out here in the fog." As she stares out at a William Daniels sea with the visual consistency of tapioca pudding, Garbo convinces us, with one of her uncanny retinal embraces, that the damp night is her true demon-lover—and that to die in the fog would be to return, finally and irrevocably, to the womb of her own superior solitude.

But the shouts that come to her from out of the fog are not the seductive invocations of death, but only the cries of an abandoned sailor. And the rest of the film details not the inexplicable workings of fate but the creaky mechanics of an O'Neill plot. Charles Bickford takes a manly stab at playing Matt Burke, the rugged proletarian. But the "begorrahs" and "mother o' mercys" that O'Neill stuffed down Matt's Irish gullet don't come out easily, and the part ultimately defeats him.

The film's third act is a hysterical, three-cornered tangle in which Garbo tries to convince Bickford—as she tried with so many of her leading men—that "I love you, and I haven't ever loved a man before you." And Bickford argues with Marion over the validity of the oath a Lutheran-born girl took on his mother's rosary! It makes *Abie's Irish Rose* look like *Romeo and Juliet*. And Dressler, who might have brought some comic balance as the meddling nurse to Garbo's Juliet, is simply forgotten by the filmmakers, if not by a wistful audience.

It's hard to know what to make of Garbo's performance in this long scene. She's either ridiculous or sublime—perhaps both. By any accepted standard of movie acting, her performance is a mess, with much neurotic pushing back of her hair and compulsive scrunching of her left breast. And yet she seizes our attention, and we watch her as we might some Japanese movie that relies on conventions totally alien from ours: we may be moved by it, but do we understand it? Perhaps we're simply awed by the nutty intensity with which she tries to bring her character to life. It's a form of artificial respiration that is almost a form of art.

ANNA CHRISTIE (1930). With Charles Bickford

ANNA CHRISTIE (1930). A scene from the German version, with director Jacques Feyder, Herman Bing, and Salka Steuermann (Viertel)

Whatever cramped vision *Anna Christie* may present to us today, it looked quite good to contemporary critics. In a 1930 issue of *Life*, Robert E. Sherwood wrote about Garbo: "Her intelligence and grace were revealed in all her silent films, from *The Torrent* to *The Kiss*. Her intense power bursts forth for the first time in *Anna Christie*." O'Neill himself told critic Richard Watts that "he was anxious to see it because he admired Garbo. But a year later he told Watts that he had not seen it and was not going to, because friends had told him it was bad."* Garbo was said to have preferred the German-language version she made with Jacques Feyder; it uses all the same sets and most of the same camera set-ups, but conveys more feelingly the mood of doom. And Garbo, in Caligari make-up, seems at ease speaking German and surrendering herself to Feyder's menacing shadows. Of the Brown version, she said to a friend: "Isn't it terrible? Who ever saw Swedes act like that?"

ROMANCE (1930)

To me, love is only a little warmth in all this cold, just a little light in all this darkness, one little minute to lie still in the beloved's arms, one little minute to forget—and that's all.

Of all Garbo's films, *Romance* is the one without a single redeeming little minute of dramatic or cinematic charm. The only spark of spontaneity comes when her pet monkey bites a respectable old woman on the ear. Gavin Gordon is better-looking as the eighty-year-old man who narrates the film-long flashback than as the twenty-eight-year-old curate who falls in love with a coquettish diva. With her Marguerite Gautier curls and her "be gay or die" insouciance, Garbo's Madame Cavillini is a very rough sketch—more like a finger painting—for *Camille*. And her suicidal self-sacrifice gives off faint emanations of the doomed ballerina of *Grand Hotel*. But these are only promises, and the rest of *Romance* leaves them unfulfilled.

It was a bad idea to cast Garbo, in only her second talkie, as an Italian opera singer. She does her best to get the speech patterns down right—with musical vowels, blurred consonants, and *r*'s that roll like the Tuscan hills—but at times the Italian accent elides carelessly into her natural Swedish, and once in a while it's difficult to tell whether she's speaking Italian or English. Her idea of Latin body movements is even further afield. She smiles, frowns, winks, inhales—all mischievously—and relies heavily on extravagant hand signals, as if translating simultaneously for the deaf.

*Arthur and Barbara Gelb, *O'Neill*, 1962, Harper

ROMANCE (1930). As Madame Cavillini

As a play, *Romance* had been a great success for Doris Keane, who had also starred in the stage hit that became *The Divine Woman.* But as Clarence Brown filmed it, *Romance* is still a play—with recognizable curtain lines, acting styles that project themselves to the top balcony but not to a movie audience, and a *mise-en-scène* that is less pedestrian than disabled. Brown consistently uses long shots when medium shots are called for, and medium shots when he should use closeups. It's as if Clarence Brown, the admirable technician, had died with the coming of sound, and most of his later films were directed not by his spirit but by his shade.

The result is a feature-length series of static two-shots instead of true picture motion, of statuesque postures instead of felt gestures. And Garbo is strangled by her role even as she is stranded in the desolate expanses of the film frame. There is, of course, the vagrant moment of inspiration, as when she holds a lock of her lover's baby hair to her cheek, and whispers, "Oh, it's so soft!" with real affection and regret; or when she kisses his mother's pearls as she would a rosary—and walks out of his life. And toward the end she does manage to suggest that it's the minister's innocence that excites her, his Christian charity that she desires,

ROMANCE (1930). With Gavin Gordon

ROMANCE (1930). With Lewis Stone

and his rejection that she needs. But the rest is desolation and boredom.

In two of her silent films (*The Torrent* and *The Mysterious Lady*), Garbo "sang"—her lips moved, her audience "listened" raptly, and we cursed the medium for depriving us of some grand movie moments. But when MGM cast her into *Romance*, not only was her resonant contralto voice dubbed by a girlish soprano (Diana Gaylen), but we never even see Garbo move her lips. It all takes place either off-screen or in a Goodyear Blimp long-shot. MGM, in an act of corporate sadomasochism, first robbed Garbo of an actable character, and then stole her voice. No wonder her performance, and the film itself, are off-key. Even the chimes from the clock on Garbo's mantelpiece are flat.

INSPIRATION (1931)

JOHN MILJAN (fervently): *You were more than my life. You were my—*

GARBO (bored and ironic): *Yes, I know. Your inspiration.*

To film *Romance* once was silly. To remake the same plot, six months later, with the same star and director, must seem completely daft. Again Garbo plays a famous artiste and notorious "loose woman" who finally finds True Love; and just as she renounces her past, her hero discovers it, and leaves her for a safely virginal young lady. Of course, half a dozen other Garbo films had basically the same plot. And sometimes, as in *A Woman of Affairs* and *Camille*, she made them into something like art. More often, though, when she played in this sort of tripe, the tripe won. The only reason to remake *Romance* would be to atone for it.

And to a sizable extent, for the first half of the film, *Inspiration* is an offer of apology we can't refuse. In discussing Clarence Brown's direction of *Romance* we declared him missing in action and presumed dead. But his work throughout much of *Inspiration* indicates that reports of his demise were somewhat premature. Where *Romance* was hidebound and stagebound, except for an introductory sequence with New Year's Eve revelers blowing paper trumpets into the screen, *Inspiration* begins in dark, dazzling half-lights and proceeds with the stylish assurance of a top director working in top form.

As for Garbo, she seems to have recovered from her bout of Italianate manic-depressiveness. She looks great—especially in the early scenes, where her fluffy hair is backlit by some William Daniels fireflies—and seems to be enjoying herself in the bargain. In these early scenes, when she can play the brightest light of Paris without too much anticipated guilt, she radiates soft-focus sex, treating her old, cynical lovers with cool urbanity, and the new love of her life (Robert Montgomery) with a smile, an interested stare, and a steadying hand on his shaking one. He sees; she conquers; they come together.

As with a few other Garbo films, *Inspiration*'s most successful sections are those adagios when she and her young man realize they are falling in love. The ecstatic rise and resigned fall of their seismic affair are nicely handled here via two long, complementary shots constructed around an apartment stairwell. The first is a two-minute-long crane shot that follows the lovers up the stairs, discreetly standing back when Garbo refuses (or postpones) Montgomery's first kiss, and ends only when they enter his rooms. In the second shot, the next morning, the lovers come playfully but portentously down the stairs and stop at the landing where Garbo had rejected Montgomery and where she now begs him to come

INSPIRATION (1931). With Beryl Mercer

INSPIRATION (1931). With Robert Montgomery

with her. The shot ends as Garbo walks briskly away, and Montgomery runs after her with tiny diplomatic steps, and she closes the door on him.

Montgomery, as an apprentice ambassador who looks eerily, and appropriately, like a young Elliot Richardson, is fine in these lovely quiet passages. It's when he learns that he is not Garbo's first lover, and his innocent rectitude turns into naive righteousness, that his performance goes to pieces. In the final renunciation scene, his clipped tones and prep-school sulkiness aren't so much understated as inaudible, and Garbo is forced to pitch her bravura technique against a blank wall.

Garbo learned her trade in the silent cinema, and she still remembered most of her lessons in the early sound period. This made her a beautiful dinosaur, an Olympian remnant surviving into the Plastic Age; and the wrong kind of co-star could make both of them look foolish. That's what happens here. In the middle of a painful farewell, Montgomery examines his fingernails! Of the many acting colleagues Norman Zierold interviewed for his Garbo biography, Montgomery was the only one who refused to talk about her. The only excuse for his criminal inertia at the conclusion of *Inspiration* is that the star and her young leading man just didn't get along—at least not after they saw the rushes.

Montgomery may, of course, have been reacting to the script, which made him behave like a pompous ass who spurns Garbo after she has left Paris to be with him in the country, and even learned to cook. But what's Clar-

INSPIRATION (1931). With Robert Montgomery

SUSAN LENOX: HER FALL AND RISE (1931). With Cecil Cunningham

ence Brown's excuse? He proved early in the film that he still knew how to direct the lights, the camera, and the actors—so why does he nod off just when Garbo needs him most?

As she nobly abandons the sleeping Montgomery to walk out alone into the snow, Brown holds the camera on Montgomery—as if he were a true director's surrogate—without even giving Garbo the courtesy of a final shot: solitary and shivering and shimmering in the snowlight. Toward the end of *Inspiration*, Garbo tells Montgomery, "I just want to be alone for a little while." Brown, it would seem, took her wish at face value—and deserted his star.

SUSAN LENOX: HER FALL AND RISE (1931)

This time I rise—or fall—alone.

Good movies have the cumulative impact of any narrative form. Maybe that's why we remember films that begin poorly but end well more fondly than those which, after a fine start, taper off into the ludicrous or banal. The tattered reputation of *Susan Lenox: Her Fall and Rise* can be blamed on its last half-hour, where the movie goes haywire. We get only an aerial photograph of the emotional terrain, as whole scenes, plot reversals, even countries fly perfunctorily by. The whirlwind pacing of the lovers' final reconciliation turns *Susan Lenox* into a two-reel comedy, forfeiting poignancy and common sense in a mad dash to beat the fade-out.

But much of what goes before is really quite good. Robert Z. Leonard, who had appeared in the first fiction film to be made entirely in California, and later studied under D.W. Griffith, knew how to telescope time through a sort of montage of shadows: a series of silhouettes, against the wall of a Danish laborer's hut, that shows the protagonist's growth from a baby to a child to a young adolescent to the eighteen-year-old Garbo. Leonard also knew how to create a gossamer mood that could surround and sustain the serene, understated courtship of Garbo and the young Clark Gable. This aura of rural good feeling recalls Griffith at his effortless best. Lillian Gish and Bobby Harron would not have been out of place in the early part of *Susan Lenox*.

Like the Sternberg-Dietrich *Blonde Venus* of a year later, *Susan Lenox* traces a steep downward slope from respectability to ruin. But Garbo always took herself more seriously than did Dietrich, and her film is the more straightforward of the two, with none of *Blonde Venus*' side-trips into baroque art direction or pre-camp drag that allow today's audiences to view the Sternberg film as an opium eater's *Inferno*. Leonard seems content with an express ride through the middle and lower depths: a miserable childhood, a lovely romantic interlude, the stale cigar smoke of a carnival milieu, a rugged climb to the top over men's desires, housekeeping with a crooked politician, regeneration and humiliation and degradation—and a happy ending!

Thus synopsized, the story sounds pretty silly. But it must have offered solace to a million unemployed salesgirls to see the most patrician of actresses dancing third from the left in the chorus line of a Puerto Sacate whorehouse—all to keep a job so she might find her man. The movies were providing a

SUSAN LENOX: HER FALL AND RISE (1931). With Clark Gable

SUSAN LENOX: HER FALL AND RISE (1931). With Marjorie King and Clark Gable

cheap vision of America as a down-and-out carnival act. *Susan Lenox* itself is something of a sideshow of emotional states, and it gives Garbo a chance to run a gamut of images and nuances.

Only three times in her Hollywood dramas *(The Torrent, Susan Lenox, Conquest)* do we see Garbo as the young innocent who will soon blossom—or wither—into a divinely desiccated libertine. Perhaps because she hadn't exhausted all possible variations on idealism and burgeoning romance, she is resourceful and convincing as *Susan Lenox*'s young girl. If Garbo was more often "the whore you could bring home to mother" (Molly Haskell), here she is every mother's daughter, papa's pet, or boy's madonna-friend.

Garbo is silent through her first scene, sitting motionless as her father peddles her maidenhood to a loutish neighbor. Only when the neighbor rapaciously tries to pick up his merchandise before paying for it does she cry out her first words: "Let go-o-o-o!" This shout, warning and mourning at the same time, would need musical notation to transcribe it properly. The "go" is a four-syllable sob that acts almost as a silent motif in the orchestration of her future suspicions about the nature of the male beast.

When she is discovered by

Gable, and he asks, "Well, you're a girl, aren't you?", her "yes" is still a keening wail—she knows what men do to girls. Minutes later, her hair magically dried and styled and gorgeously backlit, she gives Gable a grateful smile for having rescued her—and even her gratitude is tinged with fear. Once she begins to trust Gable, however, she feels free to love him. Garbo's acting turns suddenly expansive, releasing all the open gestures her character has repressed since birth. She chases Gable around his living room (upsetting furniture as she will with her brother in *Conquest*), winces sympathetically as she applies baking soda to his burned hand, crawls up his body to kiss him, and almost falls down holding his arm as he tries to walk away.

It's a good-humored performance, filled with the small inspirations of technique that an instinctive actress like Garbo is not supposed to be capable of. So *Susan Lenox* is valuable as a definitive refutation of the canard that—short of incarnating the sublimely suffering heroine—Garbo couldn't act. There are, to be sure, moments in her films when she tears a passion to tatters, or uses those two vertical frown lines between her eyebrows to express every emotion from anxiety to anger. Many good actresses, with the best direction, could be found guilty of the same excesses and lapses. Garbo, often working with no direction at all, was often a great actress. And when she was that, she was also something more. The evidence is in *Susan Lenox*—for here, she is as beautiful as she will ever be.

MATA HARI (1932)

I am Mata Hari and my own master.

The Mysterious Lady, Garbo's silent equivalent to *Mata Hari,* was content to offer a smorgasbord of spy-movie clichés, and the result was tasty and digestible. By 1931, however, Garbo was moving toward that "spirit of tragedy, where all is inevitable before the curtain goes up," as Alistair Cooke has written. Garbo could now die with impunity: her fans' eyes might be moist, but they wouldn't blink. Because of Garbo, an MGM film could be faithful to its source. The real Mata Hari (whose real name, Gertrude Margarete Zelle McLeod, was as improbably mundane as Theodosia Goodman or, for that matter, Greta Gustafsson) died before a firing squad in 1917. The rest of the film's scenario is somewhat more apocryphal.

This Mata Hari just happens to be a weary sophisticate whose malaise prods her into a German spy ring, and who discovers true love in the arms of one of her vic-

SUSAN LENOX: HER FALL AND RISE (1931). With Clark Gable

MATA HARI (1932).
As Mata Hari

MATA HARI (1932). With C. Henry Gordon and Lionel Barrymore

tims. MGM had put Garbo through so many variations on the beautiful spider falling in love with the idealistic fly that the actress could have performed this part in her sleep—and more than one critic accused her of doing just that. "Your playing was, more often than not, a highly finished piece of somnambulism," Mary Cass Canfield wrote. "You merely walked through it, like some superior and unperturbed mannequin."*

*Mary Cass Canfield, "Letter to Garbo," *Theatre Arts Monthly*, 1932.

This is not quite true. The sleepwalking gait is just as much Mata's as Greta's, and Garbo's bemused sexual irony gives her character a mordant sense of humor. Cooke described Garbo as a "superior woman whose eyes saw and discounted everything in advance." Certainly she has seen her own fate—so have we, in most of her previous films—but she allows herself to be entrapped nonetheless, a masochist among predators. The awareness of her allure is coupled with a sympathetic condescension for her would-be lovers. As a result, the Garbo image encompassed both P.T. Barnum's seductive packaging and Ralph Nader's consumer caveats. When she said no to men, it was not for her sake but for theirs.

And the manner—comic or intense—in which she handed out these rejection slips usually indicated how much she really wanted a man. When Lionel Barrymore, as a doting fellow spy, goes to kiss her, she raises her hand in a warning gesture, shakes her head, and laughs—a single, atonal note, dry and caustic. Later, after a night of recessive coquetry, as the brave Russian lieutenant Ramon Novarro starts to say something (probably "I love you"), she stops him with the injunction, "Don't speak." Then, staring at his mouth, memorizing it like the bedroom in *Queen Christina*, she says "Good night," and closes the curtains around her bed—leaving a gap large enough for a lover to look or walk through. A reel or two later, it is implied that Novarro did more than look.

Novarro, like a dozen other Garbo co-stars from John Gilbert to Robert Taylor, is here playing the role of man-child to Garbo's older woman: the naughty boy, cute and irresistible, especially to a woman tired of men pretending to be as worldly-wise as she. Novarro is the sort of lover who dashes into her room, drops a hundred roses at her feet, kneels, and declaims his everlasting fealty in iambic pentameter—a real rustic cavalier. Garbo's affinity for children and animals has often been noted, and we might add that many of her screen lovers fit into this puppy-dog mold. They allowed the star to surrender her self but not her superiority, to treat men as love objects but not as equals. Sacrifice is much nobler when performed for the benefit of the unworthy.

The Novarro of *Mata Hari* is a true believer at the Garbo shrine—no cowardly denials for him, not even when his idol betrays him—so Garbo herself makes the plea for forgiveness. Her penance has already been meted out: she is to be executed as a spy. Now she must beg absolution from the blinded Novarro. They meet for the last time in her prison cell, which he thinks is a hospital ward, and talk about her imminent death, which he thinks is only an operation. The subterfuge is carried out to the end, when Garbo unleashes a primal and pathetic scream: "Well then hold me! I won't be afraid if you hold me!" And as they part, she whispers deeply, "Goodbye, my beloved," with the voice of an ancient cello playing a solo requiem for Pablo Casals—or for herself.

MATA HARI (1932).
With Ramon Novarro

GRAND HOTEL (1932). Garbo arrives with her retinue.

GRAND HOTEL (1932)

I just want to be alone.

Vicki Baum's *Grand Hotel* never quite resided in the highest reaches of art. Her plot scheme was stolen from the fifteenth-century allegorical satire, *Ship of Fools;* her character development was predictable, her drama turgid, and her epigrams worthy of insertion in the cheaper brands of fortune cookies. But her novel and subsequent play did offer actable parts to many of MGM's higher-priced contract artists. And it gave the movies an enduring subgenre that is still profitable today, as witness *Airport* and *The Poseidon Adventure*.

Garbo's most famous film is, oddly enough, the one in which we see her the least: she appears in only two long scenes. But she was top-billed (in the ad campaign simply as "Garbo"), and her brief impression was a lasting one. Pauline Kael has written: "From her first line, 'I have never been so tired in my life,' Greta Garbo sets the movie in vibration with her extraordinary presence. . . . Garbo was only twenty-six when she played this role . . . but the fatigue, the despair seem genuine . . . if you want to see what screen glamour used to be and what, originally, 'stars' were, this is perhaps the best example of all time."*

Curiously, Miss Kael is referring

*Pauline Kael, *Kiss Kiss Bang Bang*, Boston, Atlantic-Little, Brown, 1968, p. 275

here to Garbo's first big scene—her descent from a despondent state to a suicidal one—where Garbo's presence may be extraordinary but her acting is awful. It would seem that, whenever Garbo played a performing artist (opera singer in *The Torrent* and *Romance*, *première danseuse* here), she assumed that all the stops should be let out, that her gestures could be exaggerated into semaphores. Her acting becomes larger than life, and smaller than art. In François Truffaut's *Day for Night*, the aging actress played by Valentina Cortese is poignant because she's so relentlessly comic. Of the early Garbo in *Grand Hotel*, the reverse is true.

When John Barrymore enters the ballerina's life—just as she is about to end it—everything

GRAND HOTEL (1932). With John Barrymore

changes. Garbo's despair was not convincing, but her passion is. Barrymore's Baron von Geigern is a nobleman reduced to the role of a hotel thief—the underworld equivalent of the White Russian general who becomes a hotel doorman—but, because he's Barrymore, the character is more noble than dishonest. And because Garbo is his new-found lover, the Great Profile is treated like one of her typical men-children.

Garbo is appalled to discover that the man whose love saved her from suicide was really after her jewelry. But as Barrymore talks of the bad luck that has driven him beyond the law, her face softens and lightens. She throws her arms around him and calls him by his childhood nickname: "Flix!" He is the cutest little black sheep, and she is his adoring, forgiving mother—until they begin to make love. In a single moment, the naughty boy becomes the dominant male, and Garbo falls back on her bed to receive the fruits of his expertise.

In his youth, Barrymore had

GRAND HOTEL (1932). With Director Edmund Goulding

GRAND HOTEL (1932). With John Barrymore

been for the stage what John Gilbert was for the movies: the handsome, high-spirited soul of romance. Both actors were effusive in their praise for Garbo—Gilbert because he loved her, Barrymore because he appreciated the aura of a star. In 1926, Gilbert had said: "Garbo will never act unless she feels she can do herself justice. But what magnetism she gets in front of the camera! What appeal! What a woman! One day she is childlike, naive, ingenuous, a girl of ten. The next day she is a mysterious woman a thousand years old, knowing everything, baffling, deep."* A few years later, Barrymore added: "She takes us out of ourselves by the mere accident of her presence. It isn't acting; it is something which holds us in its spell—a kind of magic."**

Barrymore must have known he had magic in himself. He also had a compulsion to spread it around, finally, everywhere but in his work. His final years turned into a morbid parody of Larry Renault, the decaying drunkard of *Dinner at Eight*. Less self-destructively, Garbo would later find herself edging toward the periphery of the *Grand Hotel* ballerina's fading career. She would never play to empty houses; but when a frustrated impresario warns that he will book "no more ballet—from now on, only jazz," we can't help but look forward with a shudder to the climactic moment of Garbo's movie tenure: when, to revitalize her image, MGM had her dance the chica choca in *Two-Faced Woman*.

*John Bainbridge, *Garbo*, New York, Doubleday, p. 106

**William Kuhns, *Movies in America*, Dayton, Ohio, Pflaum/Standard, p. 126

AS YOU DESIRE ME (1932)

Salter sticks a pin through me as he would a fly, watches me struggle, analyzes my emotions—and out of that a great novel is born.

The public for Garbo's early films knew little of her private life, and so attached to their enigmatic star the qualities of the characters she played: the superiority and solitude, the passion and despair. As Billy Wilder put it, "She said nothing, and let the world write her story." Gradually these attributes solidified into a legend, and by the early thirties Garbo's producers were consistently working this legend into her films. The tendency was evident in all her "great lady" movies (*Romance*, *Inspiration*, *Mata Hari*, *Grand Hotel*), but with *As You Desire Me* and *Queen Christina* things became a little stodgy, because the filmmakers treated both their material and their star with too much reverence.

As You Desire Me begins from a fascinating premise, and reworks a

AS YOU DESIRE ME (1932). As Zara

Pirandello play that seems intriguingly relevant to the creation of Garbo the star. Indeed, the film has everything going for it but good writing, acting, and directing. For most of the film Garbo looks as if she's simply finishing out her five-year contract. Since 1927 she had averaged three films a year; after 1932 she would make only seven more, or as many as she had made in the two years since the coming of sound. Is it any surprise that she was "so tired"? And who could blame her for wanting to be alone?

In *As You Desire Me* Garbo plays a nightclub singer named Zara who may or may not also be Maria, the long-lost wife of an Italian Army officer (Melvyn Douglas). So here again we have the *demimondaine* who discovers a new world of romantic love with a handsome idealist. But there's a crucial difference here: Garbo consciously manufactures her own transformation. "Would you help me to create her again? . . . You can only do it by believing me. Then perhaps I can be as you desire me." It's the old Pirandellian concept of "right you are if you think you are." But the film makes a droll variation on that familiar theme. The Zara character is clearly Garbo's playful parody of Marlene Dietrich. Only when Douglas has made her into an acceptable facsimile of Maria does she become a recognizable Garbo.

The film begins with one of those elaborate tracking shots that mediocre directors like George Fitzmaurice used as a cinematic introduction to the static filming of a respectable stage play. The camera prowls above and around the nightclub where Zara is singing, and we watch the rapt faces of her auditors, ending with an elderly gent who raises his champagne glass in a silent toast to her beauty. As in *Romance*, we don't see Garbo "sing"; here, though, her voice is dubbed, not by a soprano, but by a slinky contralto that sounds pretty much the way Garbo might—and exactly the way Dietrich did. And when we do see Zara, she's dolled up in a Dietrichy blond wig and black pants suit, swaggering tipsily, and wiggling her fingers as she melodramatically presses her hands to her head.

This sort of low camp is enjoyable for a while, and it's certainly in character for Garbo to retain the mannerisms until the revamping (or unvamping) takes place halfway through the film. It's just that the characterization isn't broad or deep enough to be more than a tiresome jape. The ploy may have been intentional, but it's not satisfying. And the other actors don't help much. Erich von Stroheim and Owen Moore were silent-screen mimes with skinny voices. And Melvyn Douglas was, in 1932, an

AS YOU DESIRE ME (1932). With Roland Varno, Albert Conti, Erich von Stroheim, and Warburton Gamble

AS YOU DESIRE ME (1932). With Warburton Gamble, Hedda Hopper (veiled), Erich von Stroheim, and Melvyn Douglas

immature stage actor whose noble Italian soldier was more tin than chocolate—a Nelson Eddy type with an operatic libretto but no arias.

It's easy to see Stroheim's Svengali-like Count Salter as Garbo's own mentor, Mauritz Stiller, and Douglas as John Gilbert, the leading man whose love she accepted when Stiller fell from MGM's favor; Owen Moore, the devoted friend who brings Garbo and Douglas together, could even be Irving Thalberg. But here we are reading tea leaves instead of looking at movies. Better to render a verdict on the film—the theme of Garbo's career, which the filmmakers developed with less imagination than we might have desired—and leave it at that.

QUEEN CHRISTINA (1933)

I think marriage is an altogether shocking thing. How is it possible to think of a man sleeping in the same room?

Garbo's five-year contract with MGM had expired in June 1932, and while on vacation in Sweden she read a treatment by Salka Viertel of the life of Sweden's seventeenth-century monarch, Christina. Garbo agreed to return to the studio if she could appear as Christina and if John Gilbert could be her co-star (instead of Franchot Tone, Nils Asther, or Laurence Olivier). This was a critical opportunity for Gilbert. For the past three years he had been holding MGM to its contract, and had kept making films to prove the public could accept him as a talkie star. The studio thought, correctly, that his pictures proved just the reverse. But Garbo was assured that new sound devices would modulate his reedy tenor—and MGM surrendered, and hoped.

The optimism was tinged with sadism, however. Gilbert was given a Groucho Marx mustache, and the wavy, oily coiffure of a Bronx street-gang member. And as if to parody his lingering reputation as a romantic idol, MGM cast a funhouse-mirror-image, Ian Keith, as his rival for Garbo's love. What Gilbert was to silent-movie heroes, Keith was to stage villains. His face and carriage were remarkably like Gilbert's, but with baggy eyes, a sneer for a smile, and a roué's swagger for a lover's leap. Keith's role was more fun to act—and to watch—and Gilbert was left murmuring sweet falsetto nothings into a deaf ear. So although *Queen Christina* transformed history's homely bisexual into the stunning heterosexual of Garbo's performance, the film was unable to halt Gilbert's slide to ignominious anonymity. Within three years, he was dead.

QUEEN CHRISTINA (1933). As the Queen

688-154B

Queen Christina is another one of those films, beloved of critics, that are cherished more as insider autobiography than as cohesive fiction. Its main interest comes from the implicit commentary it makes on the Garbo legend—an onstage version of *As You Desire Me*'s backstage gossip. Like Garbo, Christina was Swedish, imperious, and unmarried ("I shall die a bachelor," Christina says); a regal presence surrounded by male advisors and courtiers; a sexual adventuress who renounced her crown and sailed off to retirement, thinking of nothing and wanting to be alone. The rest of the film is a stylish but starched pastiche, a historical pageant stuffed with romance, comedy, politics, and tragedy, mixed well and served on an expensive platter: a recipe for good food and boring films.

Even the film's most famous set piece—Garbo, besotted and hypnotic, "memorizing" by touch all the artifacts of the bedroom in which she has just experienced her first and only love—has the smell of the lamp about it. Like any litany, it's a ritual. And perhaps because it *is* a set piece, the ritual seems too well rehearsed, too carefully choreographed, too determined to impress us—in short, too much like a Sternberg-Dietrich special effect. Impressive it is, but not necessarily moving. To respond to this scene emotionally takes an act of will. We must talk ourselves into loving it.

Everything else in *Queen Christina* moves very quickly, so that our eyes will catch the sumptuousness of the production but our mind won't spot the fatuousness of the script. Garbo's director, Rouben Mamoulian, changes pace only in the film's last, galvanizing minute, when Christina sails away from Sweden, the body of her lover on board, and stares out into the sea looking for—what? The camera does a thirty-second slow track from long shot to a closeup of her face, and—what makes the shot so powerful—holds on that face for another fifteen seconds, which in film time is an exquisite eternity.

Garbo herself was just turning twenty-eight—the age of her character—and one could speculate on the actress's thoughts of abdicating from the imminent threats of failure and decay. But we know what she was thinking about when the shot was filmed: nothing. Mamoulian has told us that he said to Garbo: "I want your face to be a blank sheet of paper. I want the writing to be done by every member of the audience. I'd like it if you could avoid blinking your eyes, so that you're nothing but a beautiful mask." The result of these directions was one of the perfect moments in the cinema—a summation of the Garbo mystique—for

QUEEN CHRISTINA (1933). The Queen and her subjects

QUEEN CHRISTINA (1933). With John Gilbert (center)

the star's greatest secret was that she had no secrets of her own, but only those the movies forced upon her.

THE PAINTED VEIL (1934)

HERBERT MARSHALL: *Do you know that you're the most important thing under the sun?*

GARBO (playfully reflective): *Aah, let me see . . .*

The emotional region of *The Painted Veil* covers the general latitude—and lassitude—of other movie treks into the intemperate East, from Maugham's *Rain* and *The Letter* to Hitchcock's *Under Capricorn.* Garbo herself had appeared in the Maughamishly melodramatic *Wild Orchids.* But there are some refreshing differences in *The Painted Veil.* The three main characters are adults: one capricious, one phlegmatic, one Garbo. The pace is not ponderous but measured, falling in tempo somewhere between the modern languor of Antonioni and the timeless crawl of Sternberg. And Garbo's performance, like the film itself, is mature and unspectacular.

The Garbo of *The Painted Veil* is a Garbo unlike any other. At the beginning she is a dutiful daughter with no sordid past and few prospects for an exciting future. All the radical strategies of her "innocent girl" roles are missing here: no childlike flutters or prayerful glances to heaven. In fact, though the material is not comic, Garbo brings to this Austrian maiden the relaxed irony of a deft comedienne—one thinks of Carole Lombard, or a quieter Katharine Hepburn.

When she laughs at the absent-minded young scientist (Herbert Marshall) who has come to work with her father, it's not the laugh of a stern goddess or a smirking Circe, but of a real woman amused by a fellow human being whose foibles spring from obsessive devotion to an admirable cause. And when she first sees George Brent, an attractive diplomatic attaché, their eyes do not meet like magnets, the focus doesn't go soft in shimmering sympathy, the world doesn't stop. Everything is medium shot, medium cool.

As Brent pursues her, resolutely but casually on the make, she doesn't shrink violently from him, but simply recedes with a half-smile that suggests her interest in the phenomenon, if not in the individual. So when he does abruptly kiss her, the flaring of her anger can be understated and still effective. Garbo tells Brent, "You're not very respectful," and he answers, "Not *too* respectful"—and Brent is, happily, not too respectful of his leading lady. He treats her as a fel-

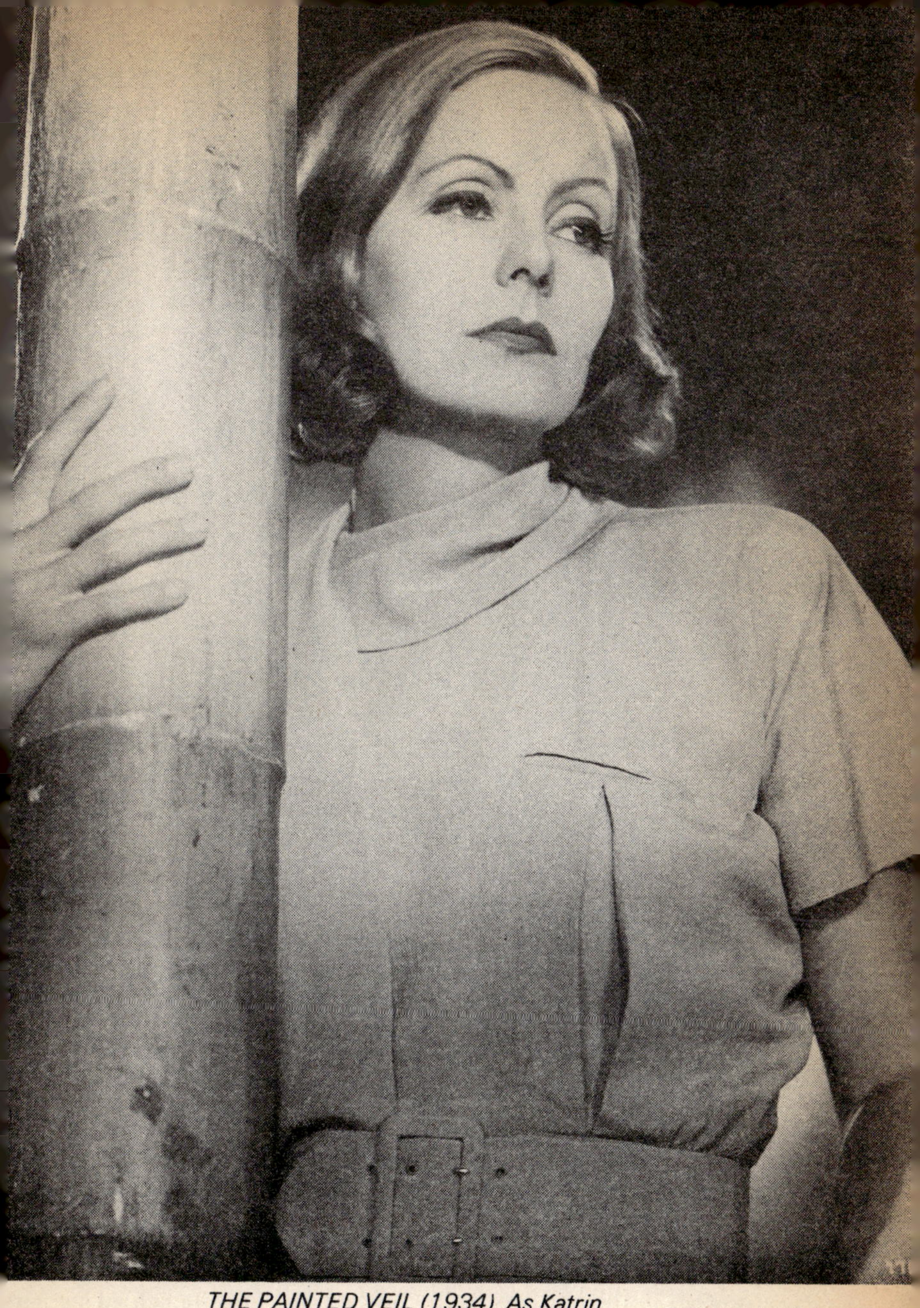

THE PAINTED VEIL (1934). As Katrin

THE PAINTED VEIL (1934). With Herbert Marshall

low performer, and not as a china doll or an unpassable acting exam. It's one of the nicest things about *The Painted Veil*: the professional equality of the actors, which reflects the director's sense of proportion.

Richard Boleslawski was an alumnus of the Moscow Arts Theatre who, in the last five and a half years of his life, directed fourteen Hollywood movies, ranging in tone from the stately *Garden of Allah* to the screwball *Theodora Goes Wild*. Boleslawski's visual effects here are deft without being ostentatious—as when Garbo looks distractedly into a window, and the reflection shows a much more disturbed face. And he helped his star

THE PAINTED VEIL (1934). With George Brent

to view her legend from an oblique angle so that, when Garbo sees a statue of the fierce Chinese god of Fate, she can laugh and say, "He looks very grim."

Boleslawski even got Herbert Marshall to shed some of his wooden pomposity. The young Garbo interrupts Marshall and her father at work and, her voice dripping with apology and accusation (neither very serious), says, "Oh, but this kitchen is a mess!" Cut to a closeup as Marshall replies, "Is it really?"—and for a moment we don't know if he is the scientist who sees nothing or the lover who sees only Garbo. Later, as a cuckolded husband, Marshall manages to look older and thinner, his dark cow-eyes more dominant. Perhaps he realizes intuitively that he can win Garbo back only by ignoring her for his work; at any rate he plays this phase of his role more as the harassed executive than as the mad scientist. Even his saintly sadism toward Garbo is always comprehensible.

As in so many of her films, Garbo finds that she will love Marshall only when she can baby him—pulling up his covers as he falls into an exhausted sleep, and joining him in his fight against a cholera epidemic. At the end, she has become a nurse in nun's clothing: less a lover than a wife, less a wife than a mother, less a mother than a loving sister. The last shot shows her kneeling down to kiss Marshall, whose face remains in heroic profile as if he's posing for a sculptor. We may think here of a similar final shot in *Wild Orchids*, and wonder that twin scenarios could produce polar opposite films. And we may understand Garbo's peculiar triumph in *The Painted Veil*: to face sexless domesticity not as a defeat but as a bracing challenge.

ANNA KARENINA (1935)

I feel pain. I feel tears. Because I'm so happy.

Hollywood adaptations of literary classics often turned out both massive and naive, like a college marching band's rendition of "The Firebird" between halves of a football game: Stravinsky sounds like Sousa, and bad Sousa at that. Garbo is ravishing in *Anna Karenina;* she brings to the film an aura of dignity and a sense of moral balance. But the heaviness of the production smothers her, reduces the size of her achievement, and we see her as we would a drum majorette from the cheap seats.

If this is textbook cinema, then the pages have long since yellowed. It's closer to what Truffaut called the "aquarium" concept of filmmaking: everything possible is shot in the studio, and the air and the atmosphere are both dead. We said that *The Painted Veil* was measured; in *Anna Karenina* the ingredients are premeasured and prepackaged, and they taste like cardboard.

To judge by his work here and in *Conquest*, Clarence Brown should have been directing royal wedding processions instead of movies. *Anna Karenina* is weighted down with "living tableaux" in static long-shot. Other shots are held longer than necessary so that we may appreciate Cedric Gibbons' handiwork and David O. Selznick's largesse. But this tactic backfires because the sets speak more of excess than of pure extravagance

ANNA KARENINA (1935). With Fredric March

—and because we really only want to see Garbo anyway. To trap her in a Xanadu of White Russian bric-a-brac is to betray a sad lack of faith in her. And suddenly we recall that Selznick was dead set against remaking the Tolstoy novel for Garbo. Perhaps this was his revenge.

Love, the 1927 version, had pitted handsome John Gilbert as Vronsky against ugly old Brandon Hurst as Karenin—a contrast that made the emotional if not moral choice much easier for Garbo. In *Anna Karenina*, things are different. Fredric March's studio portraits emphasized his distinctive profile, and he was touted as the new Barrymore, but today he reminds one more of Lionel than of John. March might have made a conscientious senator, but as an actor he was all technique and too little spirit, some talent and no genius.

To his love scenes March brought the sort of sappy conviction you might expect from Merv Griffin singing "Summertime." Because he couldn't convey exhilaration forcefully, his trysts with Garbo are lame and laughable. In March's defense, one should say that he took the role of Vronsky under protest. And Clarence Brown has said that, when Garbo saw that March "showed signs of wanting to get romantic . . . before each love scene Garbo put a small piece of garlic in her mouth." Maybe that's why, while March talks love to Garbo in one scene, he can be spotted picking at his fingernails!

Basil Rathbone's Karenin is actually wittier, more attractive and, if not more sympathetic, then more understandable than March's Vronsky. Like Henry Daniell in *Camille*, Rathbone suggests that his obsession (with appearances) is at least as honest as March's infatuation (with an apparition). The real cause of his jealousy, of course, is not his wife's passion for her lover but her devotion to their son Sergei (Freddie Bartholomew), while she ignores his stolid attempts to be warm and considerate. As we have mentioned, the whisper of an Oedipal love was clear enough in *Love*. But could Rathbone's side of the film's adult triangle have been made stronger because of pressure brought against extramarital passion by the new Legion of Decency? Or was it simply a case of one man outacting another?

In the middle of all these antagonizing forces—romance and respectability, performance and posture, Tolstoy and Thalberg—Garbo is all but crushed. It's too much for her to carry, and not enough to hold. There's a shot that expresses this feeling nicely. Rathbone has surprised her after a clandestine visit to her son, and orders

ANNA KARENINA (1935). With Fredric March on the set. Seated before them: director Clarence Brown

her out of the house. As she walks down the grand staircase and out the door, the camera tracking backward before her, Garbo's posture becomes more stooped, with all the albatrosses of the conventional world on her wax shoulders.

In one respect alone, *Anna Karenina* surpasses *Love*: the ending. The *Love* finale was impure Tolstoy, but pure Hollywood. Three years passed, Karenin died, and the lovers were reunited. But *Anna Karenina* is true to the novel (and to the Production Code). As the train under which she will soon throw herself passes by, light and dark alternate in quick flashes across Garbo's face. In the split-second of shadow her face is young, beautiful, and hopeful; in the split-second of glare it is old and suicidally resolute. By some magic-lantern sleight-of-hand, Anna's two warring states of mind are literally illuminated. It's one of the cinema's privileged moments: not a secret but a mystery, not an optical illusion but a visual miracle.

CAMILLE (1937)

Never be jealous again. Never doubt that I love you more than the world—more than myself.

A simple farm girl becomes a jaded cosmopolite, a woman experienced in sex but innocent of love. For the first time she feels the divine symptoms when she meets a handsome, idealistic young man. Throwing off the cloak of protection of her older, colder, more powerful lover, she enters into an ecstatic affair with the young man. It ends abruptly and he, not realizing the nobility of her motives, turns cynically sybaritic. He fights a duel with her old lover, wounds his rival, and leaves the country. Upon his return, he discovers that she has been forlorn and faithful all along. They are reconciled on her deathbed.

Each of these plot strands was woven, time and again, into the fabric of Garbo's films until they began to resemble factory-made crazy quilts. *Camille* is an anthology of these plotlets—and their apotheosis. Every hoary cliché has been recast and polished until it shines like a new truth. The hot tears *Camille* evokes from the toughest of critics shouldn't be confused with dewy nostalgia: the film doesn't manipulate the emotions, it respects and thus revives them.

CAMILLE (1937). With Robert Taylor

CAMILLE (1937). As Marguerite

For once Cedric Gibbons doesn't suffocate the subject with period details. Like director George Cukor, Gibbons splendidly serves the story and its star. And Garbo returns the favor with what Gary Carey has justly called "the single most beautiful performance in the American sound film."

As Garbo transcended the role of Marguerite Gautier—turning a tired warhorse into a springboard for the highest art—so does she transform her face. It's paler and more severe than before, with new laugh and worry lines. Her hair and eyes are darker, her mouth longer and thinner, harder if you like. Even her nose seems longer. A tragic mask has been grafted onto her face, and the wonder is that in her next film she will again be a vital young woman, with an untroubled heart and an unlined face. There are other modifications: her voice is deeper and the tempo of her speech is quicker; her posture is not only heroically weary but almost frozen in a not-quite-upright position. And the famous two-syllable laugh is forever threatening to erupt into a small, ominous cough.

Some of these effects can be credited to cinematographer Karl Freund, who contrasts the chiaroscuro shadings in Garbo's face with bland halftones in the background, producing a kind of twilight chic. But the hint of tragic disintegration in the eyes, the intimation in her posture that she is about to collapse in a tubercular swoon, the weight of a thoughtful passion that gives substance to every word—these are Garbo's achievement alone. It's a technically audacious performance, one that weds an encyclopedic knowledge of the craft with an innate, acute sense of a character's behavior; and it allows Garbo to play Marguerite at high pitch and with perfect precision. You feel that no other actress could create such a performance, or get away with it.

As she and her lover Armand (Robert Taylor) begin to make love, Garbo throws her head completely back, looking to heaven for assurance and prefiguring the exact angle to which her head will drop when she dies. She pushes Armand away and simultaneously grabs for him. She kisses him all over his face, then on his mouth, then sends him away, and—in a single movement—falls back toward her mirror in a sick swoon, and clutches her precious pillbox as she falls.

Garbo's performance is studded with these desperate, contradictory gestures. As she kisses Armand, her hand both covers and claws at his face. As they talk love, she pulls frustratedly on his jacket, drops her head on his chest, and cries her anguished happiness directly into

CAMILLE (1937).
With Robert Taylor

CAMILLE (1937). With Lionel Barrymore

his body. Every smile, every word is painful—she sometimes sways when Armand's name is mentioned—and we realize that each time she sees him, a little life leaves her. His function is not to help her live, but to help her die more beautifully.

It is the nature of such fables that the lovers must separate, and that it must not be the woman's fault. Enter Armand's father (Lionel Barrymore), creaking with arthritis and homilies. Somehow he convinces Marguerite to renounce Armand. And when she realizes what she must do—"make Armand hate me"—Garbo drops suddenly to her knees, felled by the enormity of her task. As she later pushes Armand away, shamming a determination to return to her old lover, Garbo again throws her head back, and for the first time we can see the strong sinews of the actress' neck: her selfless resolve made visible. Her hand involuntarily caresses his back, for the last time in a long time, and then drops, in a lover's miniature death.

Robert Taylor is usually ridiculed for playing Armand as a musical-comedy Romeo with a glistening, protruding lower lip, a crooner's smile, and a mellow, acting-school baritone. This criticism underrates the actor and overrates his role. The impossibly gorgeous Taylor is a superb personification of the impossibly sweet Armand. Instead of imitating romance, as Fredric March had done, Taylor embodies it. He helps us understand that Armand is less an archetype than an archangel—a kind of abstraction of Marguerite's last chance for love. Taylor always seems to be inhaling the fragrance of her beauty; any other air would be too polluted. If he sometimes suggests a choirboy lost in a bawdyhouse, it's because he's too intensely romantic to have a worldly sense of humor.

Camille is not a showcase for great ensemble acting. Most of it is uneven, and much of it is unnecessarily broad. The notable exception is Henry Daniell as the Baron de

CAMILLE (1937). With Henry Daniell

CAMILLE (1937). With Robert Taylor

Varville. The baron may never be more than a malicious caricature of the boulevard dandy, and his sexual possessiveness of Marguerite may never quite approach genuine obsession. But Daniell gives a quietly comic, richly ironic interpretation of the kind of man whose lips have been locked in sarcasm for so long that he cannot unpurse them even to kiss his mistress. His baron is Marguerite without a heart; his laugh is Garbo's without the soul.

To watch Marguerite's death scene as played by Garbo is to see a great actress breathe life into that soul, and then to see it extinguished with a final dying fall. Now all is conveyed in whispers—from the deepest gratitude for a friend (with just a wan smile and a feeble touch) to the strongest devotion for Armand. Only a little laugh and the treacherous cough are voiced. It's both a helpless child and a hoarse old woman whom Armand sweeps into his arms. As he pours his honeyed love into her ear, Garbo's eyes open for the last time, roll up into her head, and close forever. The camera moves in on her face, the head falls back, and the light fades to the merest shadow—allowing us to hold the image of her silhouette in our memory for a last precious second.

To write about a phenomenon such as this is to pin down nuances as subtle and evanescent as a butterfly with the net of clumsy words. It's an attempt to describe the ineffable, to attach nouns and adjectives to a state of beauty, an art, a vision caught on celluloid. Like Yeats' definition of poetry, Garbo's performance has "the perfections that escape analysis." Great acting such as this cannot be parsed. It can only be perceived, from a mortal distance, and treasured.

CONQUEST (1937)

CHARLES BOYER (demanding): *Where are you going?*

GARBO (wondering): *Where . . .?*

Even after Irving Thalberg's death in 1936 (*Camille* was the last production he supervised), MGM retained its love—or inferiority complex mingled with envy—of the stage. Thalberg had wanted Katharine Cornell to appear in the film adaptation of her successful *The Barretts of Wimpole Street*, and kept Helen Hayes on the studio payroll because she was a great stage star, even though she was not a good film actress. Garbo may have illuminated Broadway movie houses, but Cornell and Hayes had proved themselves in the legitimate theaters just off it. So to help certify Garbo as a great actress, MGM gave her a Maxwell Anderson-type history play worthy of any *grande dame* of the stage—and unworthy of Garbo.

As if to assure us that her aging in *Camille* was only an illusion, Garbo plays the first third of *Conquest* as an eighteen-year-old country girl. The cheek-furrows have vanished, the hair and eyes are light and clear again, and the smile is vacant of any predestined agony. It is the last time Garbo will play a young innocent, and she brings to it a greater conviction, a surer sense of unspoiled beauty, than she had done twelve years earlier in *The Torrent*.

What Garbo cannot bring to *Conquest* is a sense of proportion. She is cast as Marie Walewska, the Polish countess who became Napoleon's mistress for reasons both patriotic and erotic; and in any film that features Napoleon in a major role, the actor playing him must dominate. Charles Boyer dominates *Conquest*, while Garbo is forced into an advisory role that illustrates Milton's maxim, "They also serve who only stand and wait."

CONQUEST (1937). With Charles Boyer

Garbo serves Boyer—skillfully but statically. In his eyes, she is not a romantic pinnacle, but a moral foundation. As they meet in their first lovers' embrace, Boyer hugs Garbo—almost man-to-man—before kissing her. He wants her strength more than her passion. Boyer is in complete control of his part, staring down his adversaries even as he stares up at them. But it's not true that he steals scenes from Garbo. By accepting this role, Garbo obviously chose to give them to him in an act of regal generosity.

The script is a model of civilized wit, which Clarence Brown directs with a rigorous lack of style that

CONQUEST (1937). With Henry Stephenson

CONQUEST (1937). With Claude Gillingwater, Charles Boyer, and Scotty Beckett

today seems almost personal. But there is little of Garbo to comment upon—until the last scenes, when she and her son visit Napoleon in exile on Elba. Little Alexander has been her only love link with Napoleon; and now, as the deposed emperor hugs the child who he doesn't yet realize is his own, Garbo leans against Alexander, and the bond is made visual.

As it concentrates on the strained domesticity of their time together, the film becomes sad and a little beautiful. And as Garbo sails away from Napoleon for the last time, having elected to sacrifice herself for the statesman rather than remain with her boyish lover, we become a little sad too. Garbo, as a doomed dramatic actress, is receding irrevocably from our grasp.

NINOTCHKA (1939)

SIG RUMANN: *Do you want to be alone, Comrade?*
GARBO: *No.*

If *Camille* is Garbo's greatest film, *Ninotchka* is certainly her warmest. Her Nina Yakushova may be a less sublime creation than her Marguerite Gautier, but is just as demanding, for it asks that Garbo express Marguerite's tragic malaise through the guise of rigid Communist femininity. John Baxter has charged absurdly that Garbo, "in a grotesque self-parody . . . plays comedy with more enthusiasm than skill." What she really did was to make no distinction between comedy and tragedy; she played them both with the same intensity, the same soaring spirit. As for gro-

NINOTCHKA (1939). As Nina Yakushova

tesque self-parody, that will come soon enough, with *Two-Faced Woman*. If we want to say goodbye to the great Garbo, we should do it here—and not look ahead.

Garbo's involvement in her best roles was an act of total immersion, and often you can see her wading into a part, getting acquainted with it as the audience does. In her first moments as Ninotchka, she projects the dislocated impression of a Swede playing a Russian speaking English in Paris. At one early point she even seems to be reading a long line of dialogue from the paper in a typewriter. But gradually, as she did a decade earlier in *A Woman of Affairs*, Garbo assumes control of her character, even as she gains the love of Leon d'Algout (Melvyn Douglas), her political, sexual, ethical, and personal opposite. The first time they kiss, he is on top; the second time, she is—and she stays there.

There are three giant steps Ninotchka and Leon must take from their separate sides before they melt in each other's arms. At first sight, Ninotchka is the austere Communist who would deprive porters and manservants of their jobs, her Soviet subordinates of a little counterrevolutionary fun, and herself of her womanhood. Leon, the very model of a voluptuary, seems ineffective as her romancer, with his condescending tone and stale jokes. Parisian women might understand that his elegant prattle functions as code words for an unspoken proposition. But Ninotchka takes his remarks as pathetic attempts at capitalist humor—until Leon tempers his suave lechery with a little deflated humanity, falling off a restaurant chair and sending Ninotchka into silent paroxysms of laughter.

By the time Leon has talked himself into falling in love with Ninotchka, his soft-soap smoothness has bubbled into champagne conversation. "Oh, Ninotchka, Ninotchka, surely you feel some slight symptom of the divine passion—a general warmth in the palms of your hands—a strange heaviness in your limbs—a burning of the lips that is not thirst but a thousand times more tantalizing, more exalting than thirst?" Ninotchka still thinks Leon is "very talkative." It takes a kiss to trigger erotic détente between the aristocrat and the Bolshevik. Once Ninotchka has entered Phase Two, she becomes more expansive, urging her comrades to get haircuts, and opening her hotel windows to embrace the Paris of the man she loves.

The third and last step restores Leon and Ninotchka to the halting innocence of adolescence. She appears for the first time in Parisian *haute couture*, a little girl decked

NINOTCHKA (1939). With Melvyn Douglas

NINOTCHKA (1939). With Ina Claire

out in woman-of-the-world finery. In Soviet khaki she was an imposing cog in the powerful revolutionary machine. But in her new dress Ninotchka must stand on her own in Western competition with the city's most fashionable women —specifically the Duchess Swana (Ina Claire), her rival both for a treasure of czarist jewels and for a different, more desired prize: Leon. In this tug of war between love and convenience, Swana is counting on Leon's old weaknesses, Ninotchka on his new-found strength.

If we feel that the jewels will eventually find their way back to Russia, it's because we see that Leon himself is—probably for the first time—in the throes of a love so overwhelming that his seductive eloquence deserts him. He can only stammer; he and Ninotchka are equals at last. She has turned giddy and talkative, with inexpressible melancholy. "Leon, I want to tell you something which I thought I

NINOTCHKA (1939). With Melvyn Douglas

would never say, which I thought nobody would ever say, because I thought it didn't exist. And, Leon—I can't say it . . .!"

Ninotchka is wary of saying "I love you" to Leon because she had once before experienced the sensation of kissing a mortal enemy. As a sergeant in the Red Army, she had been wounded in the shoulder by a Polish lancer. When Leon expresses his sympathy somewhat cavalierly, Ninotchka retorts, "Don't pity me. Pity the Polish lancer. After all, I'm alive." Later, when she learns that Leon is acting as counsel to Swana, she turns cold. "But, Ninotchka, I held you in my arms," Leon implores. "You kissed me." "I kissed the Polish lancer too," she answers, more in remorse than in rebuttal, "before he died."

That Ninotchka has literally been wounded in love explains her allegiance to a political system in which one can lead the way for others while losing oneself. Although the script satirizes communism, czarism, and capitalism with equal élan, *Ninotchka* is ultimately an ode to bourgeois individualism. Critics can, of course, point to an almost communal collaboration between director Ernst Lubitsch and his writers (among them Billy Wilder). But it took Garbo's artistry to find wistful wisdom in the scenarists' wisecracks and deep feeling beneath the Lubitsch touch, translating the genial aura of a superior thirties comedy into the substance of acting and cinematic genius. The laughs we may credit to the filmmakers; the sympathetic tears we shed are for Garbo alone.

TWO-FACED WOMAN (1941)

ROLAND YOUNG: *What do you do in the summertime?*
GARBO: *I wait for the winter.*

Although *Ninotchka* had appealed to the critics, the public didn't exactly flock to it, and MGM had difficulty finding a property suitable for both the Garbo image and the American movie audience. Since the outbreak of war, her films had not been seen in Europe, where her continuing popularity had brought in crucial revenue. Realizing that Garbo films would now have to succeed on their domestic grosses alone, MGM attempted, in *Two-Faced Woman*, the Americanization of Garbo. She was cast as an outdoorsy wife who tests the fidelity of her busy husband (Melvyn Douglas) by posing as a sophisticated twin sister. ("I'll smolder, I'll siren, I'll vamp him to death!") The result was a catastrophe.

In the Hollywood thirties there was a writer named Norman Krasna who, pretty much on his own, produced a brash American equivalent

TWO-FACED WOMAN (1941). With Melvyn Douglas

TWO-FACED WOMAN (1941). With Ruth Gordon, Roland Young, and Melvyn Douglas

to the French farces of the nineteenth century. His films, good (*Bachelor Mother*) and bad (*John Loves Mary*) alike, relied on one-joke plots that usually involved a mistaken sexual identity. As the tone of Hollywood comedy coarsened in succeeding decades, the entire subgenre degenerated into gauzy-filtered, smirkingly sentimental, middle-class moralizing: the soft-pore corn of Doris Day and Sandra Dee. *Two-Faced Woman* was in this rancid mold. Inflicting it on the filmgoers of 1941 was highway robbery; inflicting it on Garbo was very nearly an indictable offense.

The premise must have seemed promising: sending Ninotchka to an extramarital masquerade disguised as the Duchess Swana. But instead of gracefully nudging the Garbo mystique, as *Ninotchka* had done, *Two-Faced Woman* performs a wicked, off-key burlesque. After delivering a line like "I'm a flower of the evening—a few burning, flamelike years and it will be all over," Garbo must wink to the audience, and try to gulp down her secret smile before Douglas sees her. The impression is not that of a princess on vacation from her solemnity, but rather that of a Marxist professor begging absolution for his revisionism. By treating Garbo as a joke, the film asks us to reproach ourselves for ever having taken her seriously.

Garbo the nature girl and Douglas the city slicker have nothing in common but their love. Douglas's (and the film's) real soulmate is Constance Bennett, who plays a sort of Clare Boothe playwright to his Henry Luce editor. It's Bennett who is given the best comic moments—as when she loses her cool composure by putting her hand over the phone receiver and screaming when she learns Douglas has suddenly gotten married to a Swedish iceberg.

Bennett is also allowed to give Garbo what the screenwriters evidently think is some good advice: "Your stock in trade is mystery. We don't do that any more. Frankness is our motto. We let the boys see the wheels go 'round. It seems to interest them." But Garbo would rather stop the wheels than let us inspect their mainsprings. So she walked flatfootedly through her role, as if on skis, and then sat the next thirty years out.

George Cukor is partly to blame. The director had done some inspired work on *Camille;* but here he is content to put Garbo through her athletic paces, doll her up in a Phyllis Diller hairdo, paste a Gloria Swanson smile on her face, and let her drift—and then sink. It's sad and ironic that a director so justly

TWO-FACED WOMAN (1941). With Constance Bennett, Melvyn Douglas, and Robert Sterling

famed for eliciting great performances from great ladies should, within a year, preside over the demolition of Irving Thalberg's two grand dames: Garbo here and Norma Shearer in another feeble comedy, *Her Cardboard Lover*. Neither star ever made another film.

Perhaps *Two-Faced Woman* was cursed from the start. When it was released, the Legion of Decency condemned the film, and several city police departments forbade its showing. MGM then recalled all circulating prints, and released a version that had Douglas discover early on that the "twin sister" was really his wife. Since the rest of the film was not reshot, the final version made no sense at all. We see Douglas yearning persuasively for her, and agonizing over a goodbye speech to his "wife."

By this time, Garbo must have been fed up with the movie, the studio, the industry—the lot. But now we wish she could have made just one more silly, fatalistic love story. It would have given us the chance to bid her a fonder farewell. For Garbo brought dignity and pain to her most inane melodramas; to a nasty farce such as *Two-Faced Woman* she can bring only pain. As the "twin sister" Garbo leaves her first Manhattan party, she says brightly, "I look forward to my return." So did her audiences, fervently—but to a different party, in another film.

THE LEGEND

Two-Faced Woman was never meant to be the end of Garbo's career. She didn't think so, and neither did MGM. There were always intriguing projects being mentioned as her comeback vehicles. (Movie history is littered with such promises.) In 1929, MGM had asked Jacques Feyder to direct Garbo's sound debut in Shaw's *St. Joan*, and Carl Dreyer to make a sound version of *The Passion of Joan of Arc* with the actress; both refused. Leopold Stokowski, during his affair with Garbo, had proposed co-starring with her in *Tristan and Isolde;* when the affair fizzled, so did the idea. MGM had bought *Madame Curie* for her; Greer Garson eventually played in it.

Garbo fully intended to return to work after the war. Albert Lewin spoke to her about appearing as Dorian Gray. G.W. Pabst wanted her to play Penelope and Circe in a film *Odyssey;* and Max Ophuls had made color screen tests of Garbo in Europe for a production of Balzac's *La Duchesse de Langeais* with James Mason. Other proposals sound either apocryphal or frivolous: Salvador Dali to direct her as St. Teresa of Avila; Aldous Huxley to work with her on the life of Francis of Assisi; and Orson Welles's claim that "I once wrote a scenario for Chaplin and Garbo, *The Loves of D'Annunzio and Duse* . . . two crazy monsters, degenerate hyper-romanticism . . . a ridiculous and theatrical passion . . . but neither would do it."

So Garbo the actress was gone—but her legend lives and grows. A 1968 retrospective of her films at New York's Museum of Modern Art was sold out almost immediately. When Garbo turned sixty-five, *Look* heralded the fact with a cover picture and some elegant gossip about her recent private life. There's a Greenwich Village Boutique specializing in period clothes, and called Garbo Garbs. And a recent television commercial had a young woman staring soulfully into the camera and intoning the immortal words: "SONY, for when I want to be aloney."

The film-book explosion of the past decade has spawned half a dozen Garbo biographies and picture books, which continue to sell long after similar works on other stars have gone out of print. And—perhaps the highest tribute of all—Garbo has been immortalized as the actress Karla in Jacqueline Susann's *roman á clef Once Is Not Enough*.

Why should anyone care about an actress who retired more than thirty years ago? Generally, if we're curious about a star's life off-screen, it's

because we know something about it—and want (eagerly, perhaps morbidly) to know more. Monroe, Bardot, Harlow all fit this pattern; Garbo doesn't. We know very little of her love life, little more than a list of names from several continents and every persuasion.

That's all we know, and more than we need to know. The outrage or envy some of us direct toward a star of the tabloids like Elizabeth Taylor doesn't apply to Garbo. She isn't "one of us," living out our most lurid fantasies of money and sex. She is, now, something completely "other": a goddess emeritus on lifetime loan to the world—but not to touch, and for most of us not even to see. Garbo today is a white eminence, a specter, as remote and immortal as a statue of Pallas Athena. One does not expect her to die.

What we do know about Garbo's private life indicates that it was largely a preparation for, or a relaxation from, her more beautiful incarnation on-screen. And once "Mademoiselle Hamlet" (as Alice B. Toklas called her) decided to retire for good—probably after being humiliated by the loss of backers for the *Duchesse de Langeais* project—she became the chief curator of her film image by staying as completely as possible out of the public eye.

Because we have been spared the spectacle of Garbo playing in a road-company *Mame*, Garbo doing coffee commercials, Garbo as a horror-movie gargoyle, Garbo offering us a fossilized version of her myth *à la* Dietrich, we find it easier to retain the vision of Garbo the great actress. Indeed, we have no other vision to retain. She took the advice of the Roman wit Gracian: "A beautiful woman should break her mirror early." The mirror broke in 1941, and all we have left is a star's reflection, preserved in a movie can.

That's why those news photos of Garbo shielding her face with her hands—the gesture of a shy schoolboy cringing from the snowball of unwanted publicity—seem so obscene. It's more for us than for herself that she covers up the evidence of the disintegration of age. She is protecting the image we have of her. Why should we want to desecrate it, with a journalistic autopsy performed on a living person? For seventeen years, in the movies, she was Garbo. Photographs before and after that period are really of a young girl—and an older woman—named Greta Gustafsson. If we respond to the genius of the actress she was on film, we should respect the wishes of the woman she is today, and leave her as she wants to be—alone.

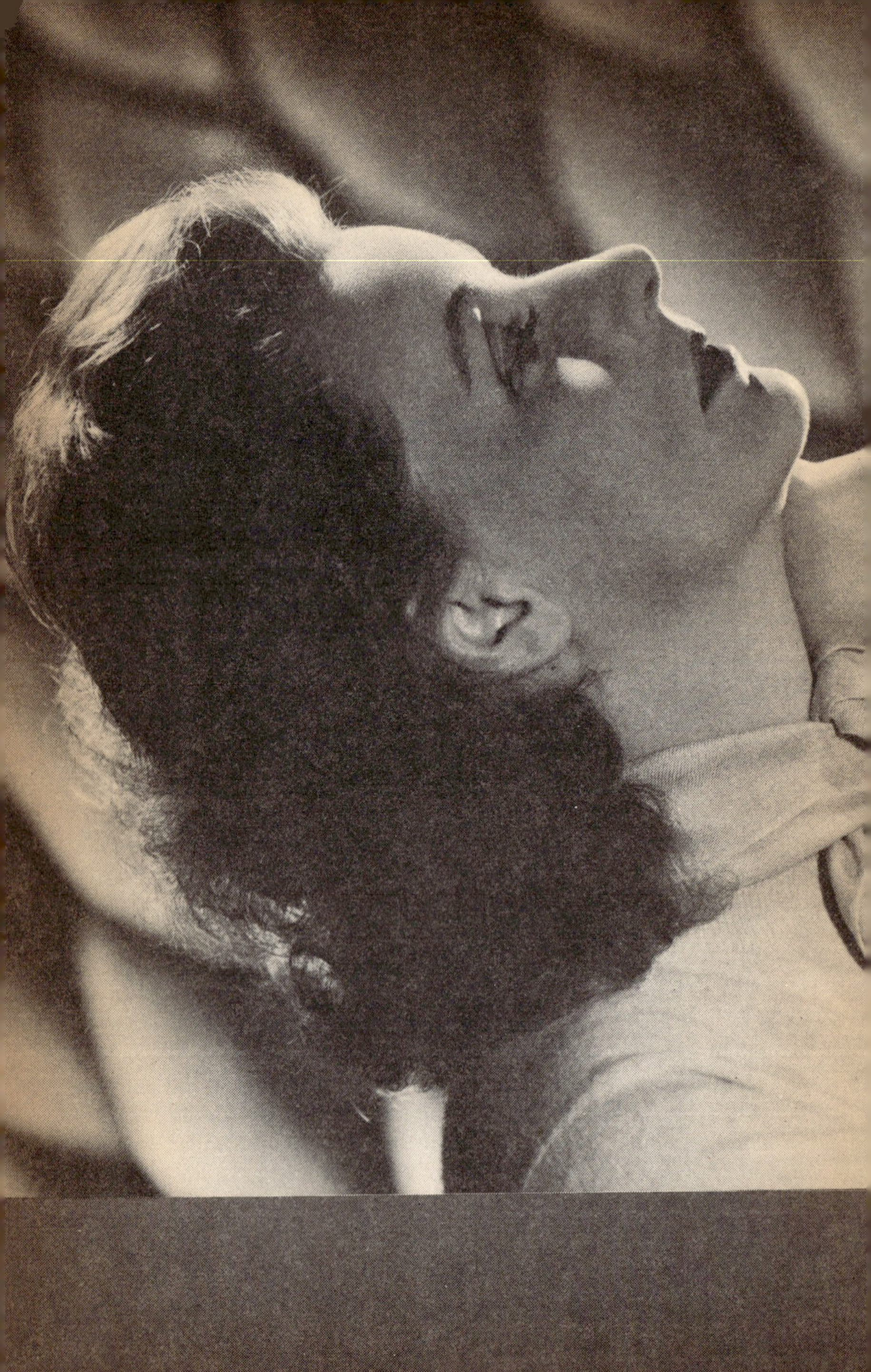

BIBLIOGRAPHY

Agate, James. *Around Cinemas.* Horne & Van Thal, London, 1946.

Bainbridge, John. *Garbo,* Doubleday, Garden City, New York, 1955.

Baxter, John. *Hollywood in the Thirties.* A.S. Barnes, New York, 1968.

Behlmer, Rudy (ed.). *Memo from David O. Selznick.* Viking, New York, 1972.

Bodeen, De Witt. "Memories of Garbo: A Fan's Notes." *Focus on Film,* number 15, Summer 1973.

Brackett, Charles, Billy Wilder, and Walter Reisch. *Ninotchka.* Viking, New York, 1972.

Brownlow, Kevin. *The Parade's Gone By . . .* Knopf, New York, 1968.

Carey, Gary. *Cukor & Co.* Museum of Modern Art, New York, 1971.

Carr, Larry. *Four Fabulous Faces.* Arlington House, New Rochelle, New York, 1970.

Conway, Michael, Dion McGregor, and Mark Ricci. *The Films of Greta Garbo.* Citadel, New York, 1963.

Cooke, Alistair (ed.). *Garbo and the Night Watchmen.* McGraw Hill, New York, 1971.

Corliss, Richard. *Talking Pictures.* Overlook Press, Woodstock, New York, 1974.

———————— (ed.) *Garbo* (program notes for Garbo retrospective at Museum of Modern Art), 1968.

Crowther, Bosley. *The Great Films: Fifty Golden Years of Motion Pictures.* Putnam, New York, 1968.

Durgnat, Raymond and John Kobal. *Greta Garbo.* Dutton, New York, 1965.

Gelb, Arthur and Barbara. *O'Neill.* Harper, New York, 1962.

Haskell, Molly. *From Reverence to Rape.* Holt, Rinehart and Winston, New York, 1974.

Kael, Pauline. *Kiss Kiss Bang Bang.* Little, Brown, Boston, 1968.

Kuhns, William. *Movies in America.* Pflaum/Standard, Dayton, Ohio, 1972.

Macdonald, Dwight. *Dwight Macdonald on Movies.* Prentice-Hall, Englewood Cliffs, New Jersey, 1969.

McCarthy, Mary. *Mary McCarthy's Theatre Chronicles.* Farrar, Straus, New York, 1963.

Sadoul, Georges (translated, edited, and updated by Peter Morris). *Dictionary of Film Makers.* University of California Press, Berkeley, California, 1972.

Sarris, Andrew. *The American Cinema.* Dutton, New York, 1968.

Tyler, Parker. *Sex Psyche Etcetera in the Film.* Pelican, Baltimore, 1971.

Walker, Alexander. *Sex in the Movies: The Celluloid Sacrifice.* Penguin, Baltimore, 1968.

Weinberg, Herman G. *The Lubitsch Touch.* Dutton, New York, 1968.

————————. *Saint Cinema.* Dover, New York, 1973.

Zierold, Norman. *Garbo.* Stein & Day, New York, 1969.

THE FILMS OF GRETA GARBO

The director's name follows the release date. Sp indicates Screenplay and b/o indicates based/on.

HOW NOT TO DRESS. PUB (the Paul U. Bergström department store in Stockholm), 1921. *Captain Ragnar Ring.* The first of two film commercials made by the young Greta Gustafsson.

OUR DAILY BREAD. PUB, 1922. *Captain Ragnar Ring.*

LUFFAR-PETTER (PETER THE TRAMP). Petschler, 1923. *Erik A. Petschler.* Sp: Erik A. Petschler. Cast: Erik A. Petschler, Helmer Larsson, Fredrik Olsson, Tyra Ryman.

GOSTA BERLINGS SAGA (THE SAGA OF GOSTA BERLING). Svensk Filmindustri, 1924. *Mauritz Stiller.* Sp: Mauritz Stiller, Ragnar Hyltén-Cavallius, b/o novel by Selma Lagerlöf. Cast: Lars Hanson, Gerda Lundeqvist-Dahlström, Mona Martenson, Otto Elg-Lundberg.

DIE FREUDLOSE GASSE (JOYLESS STREET). Hirschel-Sofar, 1925. *Georg Wilhelm Pabst.* Sp: Willi Haas, b/o novel by Hugo Bettauer. Cast: Jaro Furth, Werner Krauss, Asta Nielsen, Valeska Gert, Marlene Dietrich (as woman in breadline with Garbo and Nielsen).

THE TORRENT. MGM, 1926. *Monta Bell.* Sp: Dorothy Farnum, b/o novel by Vicente Blasco-Ibáñez. Cast: Ricardo Cortez, Gertrude Olmstead, Edward Connelly, Lucien Littlefield, Tully Marshall.

THE TEMPTRESS. MGM, 1926. *Fred Niblo* (and, uncredited, Mauritz Stiller). Sp: Dorothy Farnum, b/o novel by Vicente Blasco-Ibáñez. Cast: Antonio Moreno, Roy D'Arcy, Marc MacDermott, Lionel Barrymore, Virginia Brown Faire.

FLESH AND THE DEVIL. MGM, 1927. *Clarence Brown.* Sp: Benjamin Glazer, b/o novel (*The Undying Past*) by Hermann Sudermann. Cast: John Gilbert, Lars Hanson, Barbara Kent, George Fawcett, Marc MacDermott.

LOVE. MGM, 1927. *Edmund Goulding.* Sp: Frances Marion, b/o novel *(Anna Karenina)* by Leo Tolstoy. Cast: John Gilbert, George Fawcett, Emily Fitzroy, Brandon Hurst, Philippe De Lacy.

THE DIVINE WOMAN. MGM, 1928. *Victor Seastrom.* Sp: Dorothy Farnum, b/o play *(Starlight)* by Gladys Unger. Cast: Lars Hanson, Lowell Sherman, Polly Moran, Dorothy Cumming, John Mack Brown.

THE MYSTERIOUS LADY. MGM, 1928. *Fred Niblo.* Sp: Bess Meredyth, b/o novel *(War in the Dark)* by Ludwig Wolff. Cast: Conrad Nagel, Gustav von Seyffertitz, Edward Connelly, Albert Pollet, Richard Alexander.

A WOMAN OF AFFAIRS. MGM, 1929. *Clarence Brown.* Sp: Bess Meredyth, b/o novel *(The Green Hat)* by Michael Arlen. Cast: John Gilbert, Lewis Stone, John Mack Brown, Douglas Fairbanks Jr., Hobart Bosworth, Dorothy Sebastian.

WILD ORCHIDS. MGM, 1929. *Sidney Franklin.* Sp: Hans Kraly, Richard Schayer, Willis Goldbeck, b/o story ("Heat") by John Colton. Cast: Lewis Stone, Nils Asther.

A MAN'S MAN. MGM, 1929. *James Cruze.* Sp: Forrest Halsey, b/o play by Patrick Kearney. Cast: William Haines, Josephine Dunn, Sam Hardy, Mae Busch, John Gilbert. Garbo appears as herself in a cameo role.

THE SINGLE STANDARD. MGM, 1929. *John S. Robertson.* Sp: Josephine Lovett, b/o novel by Adela Rogers St. John. Cast: Nils Asther, John Mack Brown, Dorothy Sebastian, Lane Chandler, Robert Castle.

THE KISS. MGM, 1929. *Jacques Feyder.* Sp: Hans Kraly, b/o story by George M. Saville. Cast: Conrad Nagel, Anders Randolph, Holmes Herbert, Lew Ayres, George Davis.

ANNA CHRISTIE. MGM, 1930. *Clarence Brown.* Sp: Frances Marion, b/o play by Eugene O'Neill. Cast: Charles Bickford, Marie Dressler, George F. Marion.

ANNA CHRISTIE (German-language version). MGM, 1930. *Jacques Feyder.* Sp: Frances Marion, with a German translation by Walter Hasenclever, b/o play by Eugene O'Neill. Cast: Hans Junkermann, Theo Shall, Salka Steuermann (Viertel).

ROMANCE. MGM, 1930. *Clarence Brown.* Sp: Bess Meredyth, Edwin Justus Mayer, b/o play by Edward Shelton. Cast: Lewis Stone, Gavin Gordon, Elliott Nugent, Florence Lake, Henry Armetta.

INSPIRATION. MGM, 1931. *Clarence Brown.* Sp: Gene Markey, b/o novel *Sapho* by Alphonse Daudet. Cast: Robert Montgomery, Lewis Stone, Marjorie Rambeau, John Miljan, Karen Morley.

SUSAN LENOX: HER FALL AND RISE. MGM, 1931. *Robert Z. Leonard.* Sp: Wanda Tuchock, Zelda Sears, Leon Gordon, b/o novel by David Graham Phillips. Cast: Clark Gable, Jean Hersholt, John Miljan, Alan Hale, Hale Hamilton.

MATA HARI. MGM, 1932. *George Fitzmaurice.* Sp: Benjamin Glazer, Leo Birinski, Doris Anderson, Gilbert Emery, b/o story by Glazer and Birinski. Cast: Ramon Novarro, Lionel Barrymore, Lewis Stone, C. Henry Gordon, Karen Morley.

GRAND HOTEL. MGM, 1932. *Edmund Goulding.* Sp: William A. Drake (and, uncredited, Frances Marion), b/o novel and play by Vicki Baum. Cast: John Barrymore, Joan Crawford, Lionel Barrymore, Wallace Beery, Lewis Stone.

AS YOU DESIRE ME. MGM, 1932. *George Fitzmaurice.* Sp: Gene Markey, b/o play by Luigi Pirandello. Cast: Melvyn Douglas, Erich von Stroheim, Owen Moore, Hedda Hopper, Rafaela Ottiano.

QUEEN CHRISTINA. MGM, 1933. *Rouben Mamoulian.* Sp: Salka Viertel, H.M. Harwood, S.N. Behrman, b/o story by Viertel and Margaret F. Fevine. Cast: John Gilbert, Ian Keith, Lewis Stone, Elizabeth Young, C. Aubrey Smith.

THE PAINTED VEIL. MGM, 1934. *Richard Boleslawski.* Sp: John Meehan, Salka Viertel, Edith Fitzgerald, b/o novel by W. Somerset Maugham. Cast: Herbert Marshall, George Brent, Warner Oland, Jean Hersholt, Beulah Bondi.

ANNA KARENINA. MGM, 1935. *Clarence Brown.* Sp: Clemence Dane, Salka Viertel, S.N. Behrman, b/o novel by Leo Tolstoy. Cast: Fredric March, Basil Rathbone, Freddie Bartholomew, Maureen O'Sullivan, May Robson.

CAMILLE. MGM, 1937. *George Cukor.* Sp: Zoë Akins, Frances Marion, James Hilton, b/o play *(La Dame aux Camellias)* by Alexandre Dumas, *fils.* Cast: Robert Taylor, Lionel Barrymore, Henry Daniell, Lenore Ulric, Laura Hope Crews.

CONQUEST. MGM, 1937. *Clarence Brown.* Sp: Samuel Hoffenstein, Salka Viertel, S.N. Behrman, b/o novel *(Pani Walewska)* by Waclaw Gasiorowski and stage adaptation by Helen Jerome. Cast: Charles Boyer, Reginald Owen, Alan Marshal, Henry Stephenson, Leif Erickson.

NINOTCHKA. MGM, 1939. *Ernst Lubitsch.* Sp: Charles Brackett, Billy Wilder, Walter Reisch, b/o story by Melchior Lengyel. Cast: Melvyn Douglas, Ina Claire, Sig Rumann, Felix Bressart, Alexander Granach.

TWO-FACED WOMAN. MGM, 1941. *George Cukor.* Sp: S.N. Behrman, Salka Viertel, George Oppenheimer, b/o play by Ludwig Fulda. Cast: Melvyn Douglas, Constance Bennett, Roland Young, Robert Sterling, Ruth Gordon.

INDEX

ABOUT THE AUTHOR

Richard Corliss, the editor of *Film Comment* magazine has written for *The New York Times, The Village Voice, Commonweal, Film Quarterly,* and *Variety.* For four years he was film critic for *National Review.* He is the author of *Talking Pictures* (Overlook/Viking) and the editor of *The Hollywood Screenwriters* (Avon). Since 1971 he has been a member of the Selection Committee of the New York Film Festival.

ABOUT THE EDITOR

Ted Sennett is the author of *Warner Brothers Presents,* a survey of the great Warner films of the Thirties and Forties, and of *Lunatics and Lovers,* on the years of the "screwball" movie comedy. He has also written about films for magazines and newspapers. He lives in New Jersey with his wife and three children.